GOD'S END TIME REVELATION

Part 1

UNDERSTANDING THE PROPHECIES OF DANIEL,
JOHN THE BELOVED AND OTHERS
RELATING TO GOD'S END TIME PLAN

Elizabeth Bruce

GOD'S END TIME REVELATION

PART 1

UNDERSTANDING THE PROPHECIES OF DANIEL, JOHN THE BELOVED AND OTHERS RELATING TO GOD'S END TIME PLAN

Note on Abbreviations: AD and BC in history are abbreviations that refer to years based on the estimated birth of Jesus Christ. AD stands for Anno Domini, which is Latin for in the year of our Lord. BC stands for Before Christ.

Publisher: Book Breakthrough Publishing
ISBN: 978-1-0687249-1-6

DEDICATION

I dedicate this book to my husband Terry and

my children Teresa, Nadine and Ian.

To my grandchildren

Danye, Remiah, Liam, Chyna, Jayden and Nya.

I love you all and hope the Almighty God

will reveal Himself to you all.

ACKNOWLEDGEMENTS

I wish to acknowledge first of all the Holy Spirit who teaches us. And thank you to three of my siblings:

To my sister Christine who through the Holy Spirit was our teacher, and who started all classes asking for God's knowledge, wisdom and understanding to be imparted to us.

To my sister Avis who was our administrator.

And to my sister Winsome who helped me with editing before the final editing by the publisher.

Thank you to my niece Judith and nephew Michael who took part in the studying of the word.

Thank you to my past church sisters, Leizel, Elizabeth and Delmener who also took part in some of the studies.

I would like to acknowledge and thank Wikipedia for its source of information on world history.

Thanks also to Encyclopedia Britannica for its fact-checking source of information.

And finally I give thanks for WhatsApp and Zoom devices which enable us to study together across the world.

TABLE OF CONTENTS

INTRODUCTION

Thank you for picking up this book. Firstly, I want to let you know that I would like you as my reader to understand the purpose in the writing of this book. *God's End Time Revelation Part I* is written to give some clarity on the return of our Lord and Saviour Jesus Christ. We were told throughout the bible what to look out for with signs of Jesus' imminent return.

God gave us His promises through His Prophets, His Apostles and Kings. King Nebuchadnezzar was used through a dream by God to inform us what would happen in the world before the end comes.

Daniel was used by God to give us information through dreams and visions about what would happen in the world before the coming of Jesus.

John the Apostle was used by God to inform us what will take place in the world before, during and after Jesus' return.

We were told that in the mouth of two or three people that every word is established.

I have found the Bible to be such an inspirational, educational, spiritual and simply mind blowing book to read. Each time you enter its pages, more and more wisdom, knowledge and understanding is revealed to you.

In a time of uncertainty, fear and disruption the Bible is the only book that can answer all the questions of mankind. People's quest to know what the future holds is contained in His word. In Isaiah 46:10 God informs us:

> *I make known the end from the beginning, from ancient times, what is still to come. I say, 'My purpose will stand, and I will do all that I please.'*

Only God knows the end from the beginning. No magician, politician, or astrologer can do this. God has used simple men as prophets to reveal future historical events that could not be explained or understood.

Jesus mentioned in Matthew 23:33-34:

> *"You snakes! You brood of vipers! How will you escape being condemned to hell? 34 Therefore I am sending you prophets and sages and teachers."*

Also we see spoken in Amos 3:7: *Surely the Lord God will do nothing, but he revealeth his secret unto his servants the prophets.*

God always wants us to know. He does not want to keep us in the dark. In Daniel 2:22 it says that He reveals deep and hidden things; He knows what lies in darkness, and light dwells with him.

Jesus mentioned in John 3:17: *For God did not send his Son into the world to condemn the world, but to save the world through him.*

From the Old Testament to the new God has been revealing Himself and revealing many things to His people. The Bible is full of futuristic events that are now unfolding and yet to unfold. The books of Daniel and Revelation are two of the many books of the Bible filled with end time events. The world seems to be reeling out of control and on the brink of catastrophe and many are asking questions. Many are searching for answers in all the wrong places however.

> *Amos 8:11-12 says: "The days are coming," declares the Sovereign Lord, "when I will send a famine through the land - not a famine of food or a thirst for water, but a famine of hearing the words of the Lord.*
>
> *People will stagger from sea to sea and wander from north to east, searching for the word of the Lord, but they will not find it."*

CHAPTER 1

THE STUDY OF DANIEL

The following is my understanding of Daniel's dreams and visions of Israel's 70 weeks prophecy. My hope is that as you read, you will have some or a better understanding of the meaning of this prophecy.

The word of God says that in the mouth of two or three persons every word is established. (2 Corinthian 13:1). And so because of that, I have endeavoured to give you evidence from two or more places in scripture to help you understand the meaning of his dreams.

DANIEL'S DREAMS OF ISRAEL, "SEVENTY 'SEVENS' (70 WEEKS) PROPHECY.

Let's look firstly at the description of the dream and vision in Daniel 9: v 1 – 27:

> *In the first year of Darius the son of Xerxes (a Mede by descent), who was made ruler over the Babylonian kingdom - in the first year of his reign, I Daniel, understood the Scriptures, according to the word of the Lord to Jeremiah the prophet, that the desolation of Jerusalem would last seventy years.*

So, I turned to the Lord God and pleaded with him in prayer and petition, in fasting, and in sackcloth, and ashes.

I prayed to the LORD my God, and confessed: "O Lord, the great and awesome God, who keeps his covenant of love with all who love him and obey his commands, we have sinned and done wrong. We have been wicked and have rebelled; we have turned away from your commands and laws.

We have not listened to your servants, the prophets, who spoke in your name to our kings, our princes, and our fathers, and to all the people of the land.

Lord, you are righteous, but this day we are covered with shame - the men of Judah, and the people of Jerusalem and all Israel, both near and far, in all the countries where you have scattered us because of our unfaithfulness to you.

O Lord, we and our kings, our princes and our fathers are covered with shame because we have sinned against you."

The Lord our God is merciful and forgiving, even though we have rebelled against him. We have not obeyed the Lord our God, or kept the laws he gave us, through his servants the prophets.

All Israel has transgressed your law and turned away, refusing to obey you. Therefore, the curses and sworn judgements written in the law of Moses, the servant of God, are poured out on us, because we have sinned against you.

You have fulfilled the words spoken against us and against our rulers by bringing upon us great disaster. Under the whole heaven nothing has ever been done like what has been done to Jerusalem.

Just as it is written in the Law of Moses, all this disaster has come upon us, yet we have not sought the favour of the Lord our God by turning from our sins and giving attention to your truth.

The Lord did not hesitate to bring the disaster upon us: for the Lord our God, is righteous in everything he does; yet we have not obeyed him.

"Now, O Lord our God, who brought your people out of Egypt with a mighty hand and who made for yourself a name that endures to this day; we have sinned, we have done wrong.

O Lord, in keeping with your righteous acts, turn away your anger and your wrath from Jerusalem, your city, your holy hill. Our sins, and the iniquities of our fathers have made Jerusalem and your people an object of scorn to all those around us.

Now, our God, hear the prayers and petitions of your servant. For your sake, O God, look with favour on your desolate sanctuary.

Give ear, O God, and hear, and open your eyes, and see the desolation of the city that bears your Name. We do not make requests of you because we are righteous, but because of your great mercy.

O Lord listen, forgive! O Lord, hear and act! For your sake, O my God, do not delay, because your city and your people bear your name."

While I was speaking, and praying, confessing my sin and the sin of my people Israel, and making my request to the Lord my God for the holy hill - while I was still in prayer, Gabriel, the man I had seen in the earlier vision, came to me in swift flight about the time of the evening sacrifice.

> *He instructed me and said to me, "Daniel, I have now come to give you insight and understanding. As soon as you began to pray, an answer was given, which I have come to tell you, for you are highly esteemed. Therefore, consider the message and understand the vision:*
>
> *"Seventy 'seven' are decreed for your people and your holy city to finish transgression, to put an end to sin, to atone for wickedness, to bring in everlasting righteousness, to seal up vision and prophecy, and to anoint the Most Holy.*
>
> *"Know and understand this: from the issuing of the decree to restore and rebuild Jerusalem unto the Anointed One, the ruler, comes, there will be seven 'seven,' and sixty-two 'seven.' It will be re-built with streets and a trench, but in times of trouble.*
>
> *After the sixty-nine 'sevens', the Anointed One will be cut off and will have nothing. The people of the ruler who will come will destroy the city and the sanctuary. The end will come like a flood. War will continue until the end, and desolation has been decreed.*
>
> *He will confirm the covenant with many for one 'seven'. In the middle of the 'seven', he will put an end to sacrifice and offering. And on a wing of the temple, he will set up an abomination that causes desolation, until the end that is decreed is poured out on him."*

This is the dream and vision that Daniel had, as described in the word of God.

We also see that in Leviticus 26, the children of Israel were told of the blessings for those who were obedient and the curses on those who were disobedient. They were warned not to make idols nor to set up images, or a sacred stone for themselves and not to place a carved stone in their land to bow down before it: for God is their LORD.

They were commanded that they must observe the Sabbath, revere the Lord's sanctuary, and keep the commands of the Lord. They were told that if they did this and they followed His decrees and obeyed these commands, that they would not be in want for anything. However, they were told that if they disobeyed, then this would happen to them: They would have sudden terror brought upon them, wasting diseases and fever that would destroy their sight and drain away their life.

There were many things that would happen - because they would be bringing themselves under the curse that had come upon the earth through satan. They would be in need and their enemies would put them in captivity. They would plant their crops, but their enemies would eat it. They would flee from their enemies even when none were pursuing them. They were warned that if they refused to listen to the Lord, then these calamities would come upon them, and they would have seven times more for their sins.

God, Who never gives up on us and Who is full of loving kindness and tender mercy, still wanted to make a way for them, even though there were consequences for their sin and for their turning away from Him.

He said in Leviticus that, *"although they will not obey Me when they are in the land of their enemies, I will not cast them away, neither will I abhor them, or destroy them completely, nor break my covenant with them. I will, for their sakes, remember the covenant of their ancestors, who I brought out of Egypt, that I might be their God: I am the LORD." (Leviticus 26:44-46).*

These are the statutes, judgements, and laws, which the LORD made between him and the children of Israel on mount Sinai by the hand of Moses. (*See Exodus 20 v 2-17 & Deuteronomy 5 v 2-21 and Deuteronomy 26 & 28).*

Daniel had his dream and visions during the time of the reign of King Nebuchadnezzar. During the reign of Nebuchadnezzar, king of Babylon, the Bible tells us that the children of Judah were taken into captivity, fulfilling the word of the Lord that was given in *2 Kings 24:3-4*. During his reign from 605 BC – 562 BC Nebuchadnezzar invaded Jerusalem three times.

On the 16th March 597 BC, Jehoiachin was dethroned by Nebuchadnezzar and taken into captivity. T*his was in the eighth year of Nebuchadnezzar's reign. He took King Jehoiachin, the king's mother, and the king's wives, and his officers and carried them with him to Babylon. He also took many of the treasures of the house of the LORD, the treasures of the king's house, and cut in pieces all the vessels of gold which Solomon, king of Israel had made in the temple of the Lord.*

"He carried away all Jerusalem, and all the princes, and all the mighty men of the land, even all the craftsmen and smiths: none remained, except for the poorest sort of people of the land." See 2 Kings 24:11-15. This was the first time that Nebuchadnezzar invaded Jerusalem.

Because of the sins and transgression and the many disobediences of the children of Judah and Benjamin, by not listening to the voice of the LORD, they ended up being put into captivity by the Babylonians for a period of seventy years.

Daniel though, did not turn away from God. He was a righteous man of princely lineage and he lived from about 612 BC – 528 BC. He was carried off to Babylon along with the rest of God's people, in 597 BC, by Nebuchadnezzar the Babylonian, and he was still living when Babylon was overthrown by the Medes and Persians in 539 BC.

Daniel lived about a further twelve years after the captivity of Babylon by the Medes and Persians. During the entire seventy years in captivity that the people of God endured, Daniel had a few dreams and visions. We see this spoken of in Daniel 7:1-28, Daniel 8:1-27, Daniel 9 & 10:5-21. These dreams were given to Daniel by God so that he could let the children of Judah and Benjamin know what would be happening to them after their return from captivity in the future.

During that time there was a king reigning in Jerusalem by the name of King Zedekiah. King Zedekiah reigned in Jerusalem for eleven years and he also did evil in the eyes of the LORD. He did not learn from his predecessors who also committed evil, and so he and the remainder of the children of Judah and Benjamin were all put into captivity in Babylon. The rest of the children of Israel were already in captivity in Assyria because of their disobedience.

King Zedekiah's original name was Mattaniah. He was born in 618 BC and at the age of twenty-one he became king of Judah. He reigned from 597-586 BC and his reign ended during the Babylonian destruction of Jerusalem. At this time most of the Jews were then deported with him to Babylon. This was the last time Nebuchadnezzar invaded Jerusalem.

The siege started on the 10th September 588 BC until the 9th April 586 BC. There was a famine in the city and there was no bread for the people of the land.

2 Kings 25:4-7 tells us of this time in history and of what happened to King Zedekiah and the people. We see it here:

> *"The city was broken up, and all the men of war fled by night via the gate between two walls, which was by the king's garden. The king went the way toward the plain, and the army of the Chaldees pursued after him, but overtook him in the plains of Jericho, where all his army were scattered from him. The captors took the king and brought him up to the king of Babylon, to Riblah, where they pronounced judgement upon him. There they slew the sons of*

Zedekiah before his eyes, and put out the eyes of Zedekiah, bound him with fetters of brass, and carried him to Babylon." (2 Kings 25:4-7)

Then on the 17th May 586 BC, Nebuzaradan, a captain of the guard and servant of the king of Babylon came to Jerusalem. *2 Kings 25:13-17* tells us how he captured the people of God and took them into exile, into captivity:

> *"He burnt the house of the Lord, the king's house, all the houses of Jerusalem, and every great man's house with fire. Also, the army of the Chaldees that were with the captain of the guard broke down the walls of Jerusalem. Now the rest of the people that were left in the city and the fugitives that fell away to the king of Babylon with the remnant of the multitude, did Nebuzaradan the captain of the guard carried away. They took all the vessels of the Lord's house and all the treasures of Jerusalem they carried away to Babylon."*

On the 27th December 560 BC, after the death of Nebuchadnezzar, a new king became king of Babylon - his name was Awel-Marduk. In the first year of his reign, King Awel-Marduk released Jehoiachin, the king of Judah, out of prison. *2 Kings 25:27-30* tells us that, *"He spoke kindly to him and set his throne or elevated him above the throne of the kings that were with him in Babylon. He changed his prison garments and allowed him to eat bread continually before him all the days of his life. Awel-Marduk also gave Jehoiachin a continual allowance at a daily rate for every day until the end of his life."*

THE PROPHECY OF JEREMIAH TO JUDAH AND BENJAMIN

As well as prophecy given to Daniel to God's people, God also raised up the prophet Jeremiah to bring God's message to the people, to bring them hope that they would be set free and that God still had good plans for them.

We see this in Jeremiah 29:10-14 which tells us,

> *"This is what the LORD says: 'When seventy years are completed for Babylon, I will come to you and fulfil my gracious promise to bring you back to this place. For I know the plans I have for you,' declares the Lord, 'plans to prosper you, and not to harm you, to give you hope and a future. Then you will call upon me and pray, and I will listen to you. You will seek me and find me, when you seek me with all your heart. I will be found by you,' declares the LORD. 'And I will bring you back from captivity. I will gather you from all the nations, and places where I have banished you,' declares the LORD, 'and will bring you back to the place from which I carried you into exile.'*

Here we see the promise of God to His people that after seventy years, they will be released from their captivity in Babylon.

He continues to prophesy about this time in *Jeremiah 10 - in verses 14-22:*

> *"You may say, 'The LORD has raised prophets for us in Babylon.' But this is what the LORD says about the king who sits on David's throne and all the people who remain in this city, your countrymen who did not go with you into exile. Yes, this is what the LORD Almighty says: 'I will send the sword, the famine, and the plague against them like poor figs, that are so bad they cannot be eaten. I will pursue them with the sword, famine, and plague, and will make them abhorrent to all kingdoms of the earth, and an object of the cursing and horror of scorn and reproach, among all the nations where I drive them. For they have not listened to my words,' declares the LORD, 'words that I sent to them again and again by*

my servants the prophets. And you exiles have not listened either,' declares the LORD.

Therefore, hear the word of the LORD, all you exile whom I have sent away from Jerusalem to Babylon. This is what the LORD Almighty, the God of Israel, says about Ahab son of Kolaiah, and of Zedekiah son of Maaseiah, who are prophesying lies to you in my name: 'I will hand them over to Nebuchadnezzar king of Babylon; and he will put them to death before your very eyes.'

Because of them all the exiles from Judah who are in Babylon will use this curse: 'The Lord treats you like Zedekiah and Ahab, whom the king of Babylon burned in the fire.'"

Daniel saw from his understanding of the words of God, the time when God spoke through His prophet, Jeremiah, who would be a mouthpiece from God for the people. Daniel speaks about this in *Daniel 9:*

"In the first year of Darius, the son of Ahasuerus, the seed of the Medes, was made king over the realm of the Chaldeans."

"In the first year of Darius whose name is Cyaxares 11, Daniel wrote, *"I understood by books the number of years, whereof the word of the LORD came to Jeremiah the prophet, that he would accomplish seventy years in desolations of Jerusalem."*

Because of what he saw in the word of God, Daniel got before the Lord and sought Him with fasting, prayers, and petitions. He confessed his and his people's sin to God, and covered himself in sackcloth and ashes, praying and repenting on behalf of his people. He noticed from their behaviours that they continued to disobey the commandments of God. They were still walking in the ways which had brought the curse upon them instead of the blessing of God upon them.

Daniel realised that the seventy years of the desolation of Jerusalem that had been prophesied was drawing close to an end and yet his people were still wayward. Daniel believed the word of God and was concerned that something far worse would befall his people in the future. This drove him to pray and fast so that good would happen instead.

THE LORD'S RESPONSE TO DANIEL

In *Daniel 9:24-27* we see that the Lord responded to Daniel and his prayers for his people. *He told Daniel that He had given his people seventy weeks to finish their transgression, and to finally end their sins, and to make reconciliation for their wrongs and to bring in everlasting righteousness, and by so doing, to seal up the vision and the prophecy.*

The city of Jerusalem had been left in desolation for seventy years, after the carrying away of the Jews into captivity by king Nebuchadnezzar. This was between the years 597 BC–527 BC, before God brought to pass the fulfilment of His promises to Daniel on behalf of his people, the children of Judah and Benjamin. The LORD promised to return the children of Judah back to Jerusalem so that they could rebuild the temple, and the city, and then finish the transgression and all the tasks that were given to them. They had seventy weeks to complete these tasks, and to do what was right in God's sight. In prophetic terms, a day is equal to a year, and so therefore the 70 weeks that was given to them is the equivalent of 490 days, but in biblical terms this can represent 490 years.

THE WORD OF GOD STATED IN ISAIAH

In Isaiah, we see reference to this time period in the history of God's people - if we look at *Isaiah 44:22-28 and Isaiah 45* we understand more of what God is saying to His people through His prophets.

> *"'Remember these things, O Jacob, for you are my servant, O Israel. I have made you, my servant; O Israel, I will not forget you. I have swept away your offences like a cloud, your sins like the morning mist. Return to me, for I have redeemed you.'*
>
> *Sing, for joy O heavens, for the LORD has done this: shout aloud, O earth beneath. Burst into song, you mountains, and you forest and all trees, for the LORD has redeemed Jacob, he displays his glory in Israel.*

This is what the LORD says - your Redeemer, who formed you in the womb:

> *I am the LORD, who has made all things, who alone stretched out the heavens, who spread out the earth by myself. Who foils the signs of false prophets and makes fools of diviners, who overthrows the learning of the wise and turns it into nonsense. Who carries out the word of his servant and fulfils the predictions of his messengers, who says of Jerusalem, 'it shall be inhabited,' of the towns of Judah, 'they shall be built,' and of their ruins, 'I will restore them.' Who says to the watery deep, 'Be dry, and I will dry up thy rivers: Who says to Cyrus, 'He is my shepherd, and will accomplish all that I please.' He will say to Jerusalem, 'Let it be re-built,' and of the temple, 'Let its foundation be laid.'"*

We can see here from this prophecy that it is speaking of a time when God's people will be released from captivity and be able to return to Jerusalem to rebuild it, after it had been left desolate for all those years.

We can also see the fulfilment of Isaiah's prophecy, and how Nebuchadnezzar was brought down and his rulership taken from him - when the Medes and Persians captured Babylon.

The word of God tells us how this happened. King Nebuchadnezzar had dreams and visions which he needed help interpreting, and yet the 'wise men' around him of Babylon were made foolish by not being able to tell him what those dreams were or interpret the dreams and the vision of Nebuchadnezzar. Neither were they able to understand the meaning of the writing on the wall to King Belshazzar.

At the time, Nebuchadnezzar's pride had lifted him up and because of his pride, he commanded all of the people to praise and worship the image that he made of gold, instead of praising God. Because of this, God humbled him and for seven years he was forced to eat grass like the animals in the field, until he learned who God, the Creator of heaven and earth, really is.

It also happened that when the Euphrates River was dried because of the wide-spread drought in Iraq, the Babylonians failed to notice that the river was drying up. During this time, Belshazzar called a party with all his generals and his household, and he had them drink from the vessels taken from the Lord's house, the temple in Jerusalem. Belshazzar desecrated the vessels of the LORD, and so he was punished for this act.

While he was having his party, the gates of Babylon were left open, and so they were all caught off guard, as the waters of the Euphrates River had dried up. The Medes and Persians were able therefore to get to them easily and capture them because of it. This event was confirmation of the words of God by His prophets.

And so Babylon was captured. This happened in the year 539 BC, when King Cyrus of the Medes and Persian kingdom captured Babylon and allowed his uncle Cyaxares 11, who was called Darius, to reign. King Darius of the Medes was now an old man and reigned for two years before he died. He was the last Median king, and when he died, the kingdom was passed on peacefully to Cyrus the great king of Persia who reigned from the captivity of Babylon from 537 BC until 530 BC.

During the first year of his reign, he made a decree for the children of Israel to return to Jerusalem to rebuild the temple.

Thus, the children of Israel, just as had been prophesied, were able to return to Jerusalem and rebuild the temple of God! The Bible confirms this in Ezra and in Chronicles, which speaks of King Cyrus, and how he allowed them to return for the rebuilding.

Ezra 1:1-5 and 2 Chronicles 36:22-23 states:

> *"In the first year of Cyrus, king of Persia, to fulfil the word of the LORD spoken by Jeremiah, the Lord moved the heart of Cyrus, king of Persia, to make a proclamation throughout his realm and to put it in writing. This is what Cyrus, king of Persia says, 'The LORD, the God of heaven has given me all the kingdoms of the earth and he has appointed me to build him a temple at Jerusalem in Judah. Anyone of his people among you - may his God be with him and let him go up to Jerusalem in Judah and build the temple of the LORD, the God of Israel, the God who is in Jerusalem. And the people of any place where survivors may now be living are to provide him with silver and gold, with goods and livestock, and with freewill offerings for the temple of God in Jerusalem.'*
>
> *Then the family heads of Judah and Benjamin, and the priests and the Levites – everyone whose heart God had moved – prepared to go up and build the house of the Lord in Jerusalem.'*

The children of Judah and Benjamin returned from exile in Babylon in the year 538 BC. They were told by king Cyrus to go and rebuild the temple, the house of God, and not only were they allowed to go back, but they were also given the resources they needed to start the building of the house of God and to lay the foundation. *(See Ezra Chapters 3 & 4)*.

After the children of Judah and Benjamin returned to Jerusalem, Ezra 3 from verse 2 tells us that,

> *"Joshua the son of Jozadak, and his brothers the priests, and Zerubbabel the son of Shealtiel his brother, began to build the altar of the God of Israel, to offer burnt offerings thereon, as it is written in the law of Moses the man of God. On the first day of the seventh month they began to offer burnt offerings unto the LORD, but the foundation of the temple of the LORD was not yet laid.*
>
> *Now in the second year of their coming to the house of God at Jerusalem, in the second month, began Zerubbabel the son of Shealtiel, and Joshua the son of Jozadak, and the remnant of their brothers the priests and the Levites, and all they that were come out of the exile unto Jerusalem; and appointed the Levites, from twenty years old, and upward, to set forward the work of the house of the Lord. When the builders laid the foundation of the temple of the Lord, they set the priests in their apparel with trumpets, and the Levites the son of Asaph with cymbals, to praise the Lord, after the ordinance of David, king of Israel.*
>
> *And they sang together by course in praising and giving thanks unto the Lord; because He is good, for His mercy endures forever toward Israel. And all the people shouted with a great shout, when they praised the LORD, because the foundation of the house of the Lord was laid. Now when the adversaries of Judah and Benjamin heard that the children of the exile built the temple unto the Lord God of Israel; then they came to Zerubbabel, and to the chief of the fathers, and said to them, 'let us build with you for we seek your God, as you do, and we sacrifice unto him since the days of Esarhaddon king of Assur, which brought us up hither.' But Zerubbabel, and Joshua, and the rest of the chief of the fathers of Israel, said unto them, 'You have nothing to do with us to build a*

house unto our God; but we ourselves together will build unto the Lord God of Israel, as king Cyrus the king of Persia hath commanded us.'

Then the people of the land weakened the hands of the people of Judah, and troubled them in building, and hired counsellors against them, to frustrate their purpose, all the days of Cyrus, king of Persia, even until the reign of Darius, king of Persia."

In *Ezra 6 & 7* we see that Darius the king made a decree, and a search was made in the archives, where the treasures were kept in Babylon.

Ezra 6 tells us,

"And there was found at Achmetha, in the palace that is in the province of the Medes, a scroll, and therein was a record thus written: In the first year of Cyrus the king, the same Cyrus the king made a decree concerning the house of God at Jerusalem.

Let the house be built as the place where they offered sacrifices, and let the foundations thereof be strongly laid. And let the expenses be given out of the king's house: And also let the golden and silver vessels of the house of God, which Nebuchadnezzar took forth out of the temple, which is at Jerusalem, and brought unto Babylon, be restored, and brought again unto the temple, which is at Jerusalem, everyone to his place, and place them in the house of God.

Therefore, Darius made a decree, that their adversaries was to leave the work of the house of God alone, let the governor of the Jews and the elders of the Jews build this house of God in his place. Moreover, I make a decree, what you shall do to the elders of these Jews, for the building of the house of God: that of the kings, goods even of the tribute beyond the river, forthwith, expenses be given unto these men, that they be not hindered.

> *And that which they need of both young bullocks, and rams, and lambs, for the burnt offerings of the God of heaven, wheat, salt, wine, and oil, according to the appointment of the priests, which are at Jerusalem, let it be given them day by day without fail: that they may offer sacrifices of sweet savour unto the God of heaven, and pray for the life of the king and of his sons. Also, I have made a decree, that whosoever shall alter this word, let timber be pulled down from his house, and being set up, let him be hanged thereon; and let his house be made a dunghill for this.*
>
> *And the God that has caused his name to dwell there destroys all kings and people, that shall put their hand to the altar, and to destroy this house of God which is at Jerusalem. I, Darius, have made a decree: let it be done with speed."*

And so because of Darius's orders that the children of Israel be allowed to rebuild Jerusalem and also be given all the resources they needed to do it, it was done for them. And so *Ezra 6* tells us that *Tatnai, who at the time was the governor on that side of the river, Shethar-boznai, and his companions, according to what Darius the king had ordered, he carried out, and did it speedily.*

Ezra 6:15-16 tells us that, *"Therefore the house of God was finished on the third day of the month Adar 515 BC which was in the sixth year of the reign of Darius the king. And the children of Israel, the priests, and the Levites, and the rest of the children of the exile, kept the dedication of this house of God with joy."*

We also see that it was prophesied in *Daniel 9:25* that the city and the wall would be built again, even in troubled times.

But because they would not let the other 10 tribes help them to build the temple, this caused a problem for them in completing the rebuilding of the city and the wall.

Daniel 9:25 states, *"Know and understand this: from the issuing of the decree to restore and rebuild Jerusalem unto the Anointed One, the ruler, comes, there will be seven 'sevens' and sixty-two 'sevens.' It will be re-built with streets and a trench, but in times of trouble."*

And just as prophesied, trouble occurred. At the beginning of the reign of Artaxerxes, the king of Persia, in 465 BC the men Bishlam, Mithredath, Tabeel, and the rest of their companions sought the counsel of Rehum the chancellor and Shimshai the scribe and asked them to write a letter to King Artaxerxes to tell the children of Judah stop the rebuilding of the city because it would bring harm to the king.

Artaxerxes, after doing some searches he found evidence of this - that this would cause him trouble - because he found that this city of old had in the past made insurrection against kings, and that rebellion and sedition had been made in it. And so because of his fear of this occurring again, he made a command that the men should cease working, and that the city not be built again, until another command about it would be given from him.

Ezra 7:6-8 tells us that this happened. In the year 457 BC, in the seventh year of Artaxerxes, the king made a decree and gave it to Ezra." Then *Ezra 7:6-8* tells us:

> *"This Ezra came up from Babylon. He was a teacher well versed in the law of Moses, which the LORD, the God of Israel, had given. The king had granted him everything he asked, for the hand of the Lord his God was on him.*
>
> *Some of the Israelites, including priests, Levites, singers, gatekeepers, and temple servants, also came up to Jerusalem in the seventh year of king Artaxerxes. Ezra arrived in Jerusalem in the fifth month of the seventh year of the king, to rebuild the city and the wall."*

The temple was finished being built at that time, and the city was in the process of being built. The children of Judah and Benjamin celebrated their first Jubilee after the issuing of the decree from Artaxerxes. It was 49 years after, in the year 408 BC, they had their first jubilee and it was with great excitement.

Daniel 9 told us that in the first 7 weeks that Jerusalem would be rebuilt, but not without trouble. The trouble came in the form of the decree from King Artaxerxes.

We know that he made this command in 457 BC, which *Ezra 7* confirms. The first seven 'sevens' in Daniel 9:25 represent 7 days multiplied by 7 weeks, which amounts to 49 weeks, or in biblical terms, 49 years. (Remember that a day in prophetic terms equals one year, which the Bible tells us in Numbers 14:34 and Ezekiel 4:5-6).

And so the first year of these sixty-two 'sevens' (7 days multiplied by 62 weeks) would equal 434 weeks (which would be 434 years), which would be the time of the first Jubilee celebration for the children of Israel. This was a special Jubilee for them, because it was after their exile. They were now free and they were able to live in the city of Jerusalem again. Both Jerusalem and its wall were now rebuilt. These numbers are also significant in the Bible as Jesus told us that we should forgive our brothers and sisters 490 times in a day if they ask for our forgiveness.

We see Jesus talk about this in the gospels, in Matthew 18:21-22 where it says, *"Then Peter came to Jesus and asked, 'Lord, how many times shall I forgive my brother when he sins against me? Up to seven times?' Jesus answered, 'I tell you, not seven times, but seventy-seven times.'*

The children of Israel were given 490 years to rebuild the city, the streets, and the walls of Jerusalem. During this time, they were to finish the transgressions, and to make an end of their sins, and also to make reconciliation for their wrongdoing, to bring in everlasting righteousness, to seal up the vision and prophecy, and to anoint the Most Holy.

The Lord promised Daniel, in *Daniel 9*, after Daniel had been pleading for his sins and the sins of his people, that he was giving his people 490 years to make their wrongs right. But unfortunately, after a while the children of Israel, after returning from exile, still fell back into their bad habits by constantly forsaking the commandments of God, of His statutes, and His laws. They did not make an end of their sins; they just kept on transgressing.

From 457 BC to 27AD, the children of Israel were to prepare for the coming of the Anointed One, but then they fell back into their usual sin. Because of that, they were not able, without Christ, to make reconciliation for their iniquity nor were they able to bring in everlasting righteousness. They were not prepared for the Anointed One's coming.

However, The Anointed One was born during this time span. The time had come when Jesus, the Most Holy was to be anointed. This took place at his baptism when He was about 30 years old.

The book of *Luke 3:21-23* states:

> *"When all the people were being baptised, Jesus was baptised too. And as he was praying, heaven was opened.*
>
> *And the Holy Spirit descended on him in bodily form like a dove. And a voice came from heaven: 'You are my Son, whom I love; with you I am well pleased.'*

Now Jesus himself was about thirty years old, when he began his ministry. He was the son, so it was thought of Joseph, the son of Heli."

We see that Jesus was anointed at his baptism, when the Holy Ghost descended on Him as a dove from heaven, and when God the Father announced, 'Thou art my beloved Son in whom I am well pleased.' Here the Trinity all meet at the baptism of Jesus: Jesus the Son, The Holy Spirit, and God the Father.

We now have the countdown of the last three and a half years of Jesus' life.

Daniel 9:26a says to us that, "After sixty-nine 'sevens' the Anointed One will be cut off and will have nothing."

We have now come to the time period of the last biblical 'week' of the 70 weeks prophecy given to Daniel. Jesus, after his baptism, has now started his ministry which lasted for three and a half years. After that, he would be cut off, but not for any sin that He had done.

At the beginning of Jesus' ministry, he went into the desert after his baptism for 40 days and 40 nights to be tempted by the devil. *(See Matthew 4:1-11).*

From *Matthew Chapter 5 – 7*, after His temptation and His Sermon on the Mount, Jesus chose and began to train his twelve disciples.

> *"Their names are Simon, who is called Peter, Andrew his brother, James the son of Zebedee, and John his brother, Phillip, Bartholomew, Thomas, Matthew the publican, James the son of Alphaeus, and Lebbaeus, whose surname was Thaddaeus, Simon the Canaanite, and Judas Iscariot, who also betrayed him." (see Matthew 10:1-4).*

We know that Jesus gave power to these 12 disciples of His that He chose and raised up:

To these twelve disciples Jesus gave the power to heal the sick, raise the dead, cleanse those who had leprosy, and drive out demons. He sent them forth, and commanded them, saying, *"Go not into the way of the Gentiles, and into any city of the Samaritans enter not: but go rather to the lost sheep of Israel. As you, Go, preach this message. 'The kingdom of heaven is near'". (Matthew 10:5-6).*

At that time, the disciples were sent only to the lost sheep of Israel, not to any other race or people. They were told not to go to any other nations, and this is because the time span of the 490 years for the children of Judah and Benjamin was not yet completed. They were still within the last week of the 70 weeks prophecy.

Jesus, during his ministry, went through three Passovers. The first one was after the time of the marriage in Cana of Galilee, where he performed his first miracle by turning the water into wine *(See John 2:13).*

> *"And the Jews Passover was at hand, and Jesus went up to Jerusalem. And He drove out all those who were selling oxen and sheep and doves, and the money changers out of the temple."*

The second Passover is mentioned in *John 6:1-3:*

> *"Sometime after this, Jesus crossed to the far shore of the sea of Galilee, (that is the sea of Tiberias).*
>
> *And a great crowd of people followed him because they saw the miraculous signs He had performed on the sick. Then Jesus went up on a mountainside and sat down with his disciples. The Jewish Passover Feast was near."*

The countdown to the third Passover is mentioned in *John 12:1. Six days before the Passover, Jesus arrived at Bethany, where Lazarus lived, whom Jesus had raised from the dead.*

Just before the Feast of the Passover, *John 13:1-11* gave the following account:

"It was just before the Passover Feast, Jesus knew that the time had come for Him to leave this world and go to the Father. Having loved his own who were in the world, He now showed them the full extent of his love. The evening meal was being served, and the devil had already prompted Judas Iscariot, son of Simon, to betray Jesus. Jesus knew that the Father had put all things under his power, and that he had come from God, and was returning to God.

So, he got up from the meal, took off his outer clothing, and wrapped a towel around his waist.

After that He poured water into a basin, and began to wash the disciples' feet, drying them with the towel that was wrapped around Him.

He came to Simon Peter, who said to him, "Lord, are you going to wash my feet?"

Jesus replied, "You do not realise now what I am doing, but later you will understand."

No, "said Peter, "you shall never wash my feet." Jesus answered, "Unless I wash you, you have no part with me."

Then, Lord," Simon Peter replied, not just my feet, my hands and my head as well."

Jesus answered, "A person who has had a bath needs only to wash his feet; his whole body is clean. And you are clean, though not every one of you."

For He knew who was going to betray Him, and that was why he said not everyone was clean."

Jesus was and is our Passover Lamb, for during the meal where He broke bread, and gave to His disciples to eat, and gave them wine to drink, He told them that the bread was His body, that had been broken for the sins of the world and the wine was His blood that was shed for many for the remission of sin. After this meal called the Lord's supper, there was no longer any need for lamb, sheep, goats, or birds to be slaughtered as an atonement for sin.

Jesus' death at Calvary on the cross was the full atonement for sin. Jesus was about to be cut off or killed, but not for Himself. This time span was about three and half years into His ministry. *Daniel 9:27a* wrote, *"He will confirm a covenant with many for one 'seven' in the middle of the 'seven' he will put an end to sacrifice and offering."*

The children of Judah and Benjamin were by this time to finish the transgression and make an end of sins, by choosing Jesus Christ the Most Holy one to make reconciliation for iniquity and to bring in everlasting righteousness, but they rejected the Anointed One instead.

That was all they needed to do - to prepare for Him and to accept Him as their Lord. They were supposed to be preparing for the Anointing of the most Holy One, but instead they killed Him.

John 1:11-14 said,

> *"He came to that which was His own, but His own did not receive Him. To those who believed in His name, He gave the right to become the children of God – children born not of natural descent, nor of human decision or a husband's will, but born of God. The Word became flesh and made His dwelling among us. We have seen His glory, the glory of the One and Only who came from the Father, full of grace and truth."*

Matthew 27:50-51a also gives us an account of Jesus' death. It states,

> *"And when Jesus had cried out again with a loud voice, he gave up His spirit. At that moment the curtain of the temple was torn in two from the top to the bottom."*

At the death of Jesus, He caused the sacrifice and offerings to cease. There was no longer any need for them. Jesus has now become our High Priest, the sacrificial Lamb, and the eternal King. There is, therefore, no longer need for animal sacrifices; it has now been abolished.

Hebrews 1:8-9 shows us Jesus as the everlasting King:

> *"But about the Son he says, 'Your throne, O God, will last for ever and ever, and righteousness will be the sceptre of thy kingdom. You have loved righteousness and hated wickedness; therefore God, your God, has set you above your companions by anointing you with the oil of joy.'"*

Hebrews 8:1-13 shows Jesus being the everlasting High Priest, who made atonement once and for all for the world.

> *"The point of what we are saying is this: We do have such a high priest, who sat down at the right hand of the throne of the Majesty in heaven, and who serves in the sanctuary, the true tabernacle set up by the Lord, not by man.*
>
> *Every high priest is appointed to offer both gifts and sacrifices, and so it was necessary for this one also to have something to offer. If he were on earth, he would not be a priest, for there are already men who offer the gifts prescribed by the law.*

They serve at a sanctuary that is a copy and shadow of what is in heaven. This is why Moses was warned when he was about to build the tabernacle: for, *'See to it that you make everything according to the pattern shown to you on the mountain.'*

But the ministry Jesus has received is as superior to theirs as the covenant of which He is mediator is superior to the old one, and it is founded on better promises.

For if there had been nothing wrong with that first covenant, no place would have been sought for another.

But God found fault with the people and said: 'The time is coming, declares the Lord, when I will make a new covenant with the house of Israel and with the house of Judah. It will not be like the covenant I made with their forefathers when I took them by the hand to lead them out of Egypt, because they did not remain faithful to my covenant, and I turned away from them,' declares the Lord.

'This is the covenant I will make with the house of Israel after that time,' declares the Lord. 'I will put my laws in their minds and write them in their hearts. I will be their God, and they will be My people. No longer will a man teach his neighbour, or a man his brother, saying, "Know the Lord," because they will all know me, from the least of them to the greatest. For I will forgive their wickedness and remember their sins no more.'

By calling this covenant 'new', He has made the first one obsolete; and what is obsolete, and ageing will soon disappear."

Hebrews 9:24-28 continues the story of Christ our Mediator and our Intercessor's work in heaven on our behalf:

> *"For Christ did not enter a man-made sanctuary that was only a copy of the true one; He entered heaven itself, now to appear for us in God's presence. Nor did He enter heaven to offer himself again and again, the way the high priest enters the Most Holy Place every*

year with blood that is not his own. Then Christ would have to suffer many times since the creation of the world. But now He has appeared once for all at the end of the ages to do away with sin by the sacrifice of Himself. Just as man is destined to die once, and after that face judgement.

So, Christ was sacrificed once to take away the sins of many people; and He will appear a second time, not to bear sin, but to bring salvation to those who are waiting for Him."

During the last remaining three and a half years of the 70 weeks prophecy, after the resurrection of Jesus, before He was Ascended up into heaven, He told His disciples to go and wait in Jerusalem until they would be endued with power from on high *(See Luke 24:49-53).*

The confirmation of this promise was fulfilled in *Acts chapter 2* which says:

Acts 2:1-11:

"When the day of Pentecost came, they were all together in one place. Suddenly a sound like the blowing of a violent wind came from heaven and it filled the house where they were sitting. They saw what seemed to be tongues of fire that separated and came to rest on each of them.

All of them were filled with the Holy Spirit, and began to speak in other tongues, as the Spirit enabled them. Now they were staying in Jerusalem, God fearing Jews from every nation under heaven. When they heard the sound, a crowd came together in bewilderment, because each one heard them speaking in his own language.

Utterly amazed, they asked: 'Are not all these men speak Galileans? Then how is it that each of us hears them in our own

> *native language? Parthians, and Medes, and Elamites, residents of Mesopotamia, Judea, and Cappadocia, Pontus, and Asia. Phrygia, and Pamphylia, Egypt and in the parts of Libya near Cyrene; visitors from Rome. Both Jews and converts to Judaism: Cretans and Arab - we hear them declaring the wonderful words of God in our own tongues!'"*

After this outpouring of the Holy Spirit on the disciples, the gospel started to spread all over the world. Those who heard the words of God accepted and confessed their sins, were baptised, and carried the words of God with them back to their native countries.

The disciples were then dispersed all over the world, preaching the gospel first only to the Jews, because the time span of the 70th week was not yet fully accomplished.

The end of the seventy weeks prophecy took place at the death of Steven, after He spoke to them about their wicked ways. This was three and a half years after the resurrection of Jesus, and so this completed the final seven years of the prophecy, as told to us in *Acts 7:51-60* where Steven says to them :

> *"'You stiff-necked people with uncircumcised hearts and ears! You are just like your fathers: You always resist the Holy Spirit. Was there ever a prophet your fathers did not persecute? They even killed those who predicted the coming of the Righteous One. And now you have betrayed and murdered Him. You who have received the law that was put into effect through angels but have not obeyed it.'*

When they heard this, they were furious and gnashed their teeth at him. But Steven, full of the Holy Spirit, looked up to heaven and saw the glory of God, and Jesus standing on the right hand of God.

> *'Look,' he said, 'I see the heaven open and the Son of man standing at the right hand of God.'*
>
> *At this they covered their ears and, yelling at the top of their voices, they all rushed at him, dragged him out of the city and began to stone him. Meanwhile, the witnesses laid down their clothes at the feet of a young man named Saul. While they were stoning him, Stephen prayed, 'Lord Jesus, receive my spirit.'*
>
> *Then he fell on his knees and cried out, 'Lord, do not hold this sin against them.' When he said this, he fell asleep in death."*

We have now come to the end of the seventy weeks prophecy time span, and we can now see that the gospel can now go to other nations and has spread to the Samaritan, and also to the Gentiles.

THE GOSPEL PREACHED TO THE SAMARITANS AND GENTILES

Acts 8:4-8 tells us that,

> *"Those who had been scattered preached the word wherever they went. Philips went down to the city in Samaria and proclaimed Christ there. When the crowds heard Philip and saw the miraculous signs he did, they all paid close attention to what he said. With shrieks, evil spirits came out of many paralytics and cripples were healed. So, there was great joy in that city."*

Philip preached to the Samaritans, and then Saul, who was named Paul the Apostle, was chosen by Jesus to take the gospel to the Gentiles. *(See Acts 9:1-16).*

In *Galatians 1:11-18*, Paul the apostle talks about how God called him to preach the gospel to the Gentiles:

> *"I want you to know, brothers, that the gospel I preached is not something that man made up. I did not receive it from any man, nor was I taught it; rather I received it by revelation from Jesus Christ. For you have heard of my previous way of life in Judaism, how intensely I persecuted the church of God, and tried to destroy it.*
>
> *I was advancing in Judaism and was extremely zealous for the traditions of my fathers. But when God, who set me apart from my birth, and called me by His grace, was pleased to reveal His son in me so that I might preach him among the Gentiles, I did not consult any man.*
>
> *Nor did I go up to Jerusalem to see those who were apostles before I was, but I went immediately into Arabia and later returned to Damascus. Then after three years I went up to Jerusalem with Peter and stayed with Him for fifteen days."*

The gospel was now spread all over the world, and everyone was given access to the gospel, Jews, Samaritans, and Gentiles - all who will accept the free gifts of salvation, through Jesus Christ our Lord.

SCRIPTURES RELATED TO THE END OF DANIEL'S 70 WEEKS PROPHECY

We shall now look at scriptures which relate to the end of Daniel's 70 weeks prophecy - the last part of the sixty-two 'sevens' plus seven 'sevens' and seven prophecy which relates to the future, and the desolation of Jerusalem and the temple, fulfilled in 70 AD.

Daniel 9:26b-27b tells us:

> *"The people of the ruler who will come will destroy the city and the sanctuary. The end will come like a flood: War will continue until the end, and desolation has been decreed. And on the wing of the*

> *temple, he will set an abomination that causes desolation, until the end that is decreed is poured out on him."*

In the book of *John 14:30*, Jesus said to his disciples, *"I will not speak with you much longer, for the prince of this world is coming. He has no hold on me."*

There was a time of destruction that was pronounced in Jerusalem because of their rejection of the Anointed One and in fact they crucified Him. We see from the word of God that before His death Jesus wept over Jerusalem because they did not know the time of their visitation or destruction. *(see Luke 19:41-44).*

This time spoken of is further confirmed in *Matthew* where in *Chapter 23:33-39* it states:

> *"You snakes! You brood of vipers! How will you escape being condemned to hell? Therefore, I am sending you prophets, and wise men and teachers. Some of them you will kill and crucify; others you will flog in your synagogues and pursue from town to town. And so, upon you will come all the righteous blood that has been shed on the earth, from the blood of righteous Abel to the blood of Zachariah's son of Barakiah, whom you murdered between the temple and the altar. I tell you the truth, all this will come upon this generation.*
>
> *O Jerusalem, Jerusalem, you who kill the prophets and stone those sent to you, how often would I longed to gather your children together, as a hen gathers her chicks under her wings, but you were not willing. Look, your house is left to you desolate. For I tell you, you will not see me again until you say, 'Blessed, is he who comes in the name of the Lord.'"*

Then *Luke 21:5-6 and 20-22* also speaks of this time:

> *"Some of his disciples were remarking about how the temple was adorned with beautiful stones and with gifts dedicated to God. But Jesus said, 'As for what you see here, the time will come when not one stone will be left on another; every one of them will be thrown down. When you see Jerusalem surrounded by armies, you will know that its desolation is near. Then let those who are in Judea flee to the mountains, let those in the city get out, and let those in the country not enter the city. For this is the time of punishment in fulfilment of all that has been written.'"*

JERUSALEM UNDER SIEGE

The siege of Jerusalem by the 9th August 70 AD was the decisive event of the first Jewish-Roman war, in which the Roman army had breached the final defences and massacred much of the remaining population. They also destroyed the second temple. The Western Wall, the only existing trace of the second temple, remains a site of prayer and pilgrimage.

The loss of the temple for a second time is still mourned by Jews during the fast of Tisha B'av. Rome celebrated the fall of Jerusalem by erecting the triumphal Arch of Titus. The Roman sack of Jerusalem and the Temple still stands in Rome.

CHAPTER 2

THE STUDY OF NEBUCHADNEZZAR: DANIEL AND REVELATION

This chapter's study is of the dreams of King Nebuchadnezzar, and an understanding of the interpretation of them and that time of history from the books of Daniel and Revelation in the Bible.

King Nebuchadnezzar had a dream. When he woke up, he couldn't remember his dream so he called for his wise men and astrologers to explain to him what the dream was, and to give him the interpretation of his dream. They could not tell him a dream that he himself could not tell them. They felt that he was being unreasonable to make such a request of them. And so when they failed to tell him the dream and its interpretation, he made a decree, ordering for them to be executed and to die.

When Arioch the executioner was about to carry out the king's order, Daniel, a Jewish slave from Judah, intervened and made a request to the executioner for him to be given time to reveal the dream. Daniel and his three friends, who were also slaves at the time, decided to pray to God, the Creator of the earth, and ask Him what the dream meant. God answered their prayers and revealed the dream to Daniel, as well as giving him revelation into its meaning.

Daniel had a dream and saw a vision while he was in bed. He wrote down his dreams and visions and then shared them with others. In his vision he saw four winds of heaven blowing upon the great sea. He also saw four great beasts that came up from the sea, each one different to the other.

John the Revelator also had a dream of a beast that he saw rising from the sea, having seven heads and ten horns, and upon the beast's horns were ten crowns, and upon his heads was the name of blasphemy. So from these two places in the Bible, both in Daniel and also in Revelation where John had a similar vision, we can deduce that the Bible is telling us about this vision and its meaning in these places.

The dreams of Nebuchadnezzar and Daniel, and the dream and vision of John all relate to events that are due to occur in the world before the return of Jesus and then also after His return. This period in the world is known as the Last Days and the Coming of Jesus, is called Judgement Day.

NEBUCHADNEZZAR'S DREAM, FORETOLD BY DANIEL

Daniel 2:31-35 tells us this,

> *"You looked, O king, and there before you stood a large image, this great statue – an enormous, dazzling statue, awesome in appearance. The head of the statue was made of pure gold, his chest and arms of silver, its belly, and thighs of bronze, its legs of iron, its feet partly of iron and partly of baked clay.*
>
> *While you were watching, a rock was cut out, but not by human hands. It struck the statue on its feet of iron and clay and smashed them.*

Then the iron, the clay, the bronze, the silver, and the gold were broken to pieces at the same time and became like the chaff on a threshing-floor in the summer. The wind swept them away without leaving a trace. But the rock that struck the statue became a huge mountain and filled the whole earth."

DANIEL'S INTERPRETATION OF NEBUCHADNEZZAR'S DREAM

Daniel successfully interprets the dream for King Nebuchadnezzar, and *Daniel 2:36-45* tells us the interpretation that he gave to the king:

"This was the dream, and now we will interpret it for the king. You, O king, are the king of kings. The God of heaven has given you dominion and power and might and glory: in your hands he has placed mankind and the beasts of the field and the birds of the air. Wherever they live, he has made you ruler over them all. You are that head of gold. After you, another kingdom will rise, inferior to yours: Next, a third kingdom, one of bronze, will rule over the whole earth.

Finally, there will be a fourth kingdom, strong as iron - for iron breaks and smashes everything - and as iron that breaks things to pieces, so it will crush and break all the others.

Just as you saw that the feet and toes were partly of baked clay and partly of iron, so this will be a divided kingdom; yet it will have some of the strength of the iron in it, even as you saw iron mixed with clay. As the toes were partly iron, and partly clay, the kingdom will be partly strong, and partly brittle.

And just as you saw, the iron mixed with baked clay, so the people will be a mixture and will not remain united, any more than iron mixes with clay.

In the time of those kings, the God of heaven will set up a kingdom that will never be destroyed, nor will it be left to other people. It will crush all those kingdoms and bring them to an end, but it will itself endure forever. This is the meaning of the vision of the rock cut out of a mountain, but not by human hands – a rock that broke the iron, the bronze, the clay, the silver, and the gold to pieces. The great God has shown the king what will take place in the future. The dream is true, and the interpretation is trustworthy."

The word of God tells us that in the mouth of two or three people or witnesses that every word is established. *(Matthew 18:16b)*. So based on this, we can confidently know what God was saying in these bible verses.

DANIEL'S DREAM AND VISIONS

Daniel 7:1-14 tells us about Daniel's dream and his visions:

"In the first year of Belshazzar, king of Babylon, Daniel had a dream and visions passed through his mind as he was lying on his bed. He wrote down the substance of his dream. Daniel said: 'In my vision at night, I looked, and there were the four winds of heaven churning up the great sea. Four great beasts, each different from the others, came up from the sea. The first was like a lion, and it had the wings of an eagle. I watched until its wings were torn off and it was lifted from the ground so that it stood on two feet like a man, and the heart of a man was given to it. And there before me was a second beast, which looked like a bear. It was raised up on one of its sides, and it had three ribs in the mouth between its teeth. It was told, 'Get up and eat your fill of flesh!'

After that, I looked, and there before me was another beast, one that looked like a leopard. And on its back, it had four wings like those of a bird. This beast had four heads, and it was given authority to rule. After that, in my vision at night I looked, and there before me was a fourth beast - terrifying and frightening and very powerful. It had large iron teeth: it crushed and devoured its victims and trampled underfoot whatever was left. It was different from all the former beasts, and it had ten horns.

While I was thinking about the horns, there before me was another horn, a little one, which came up among them; and three of the first horns were plucked and uprooted before it. This horn had eyes like the eyes of a man and a mouth that spoke boastfully.

As I looked, thrones were in place, and the Ancient of days took his seat. His clothing was as white as snow; the hair of his head was white like wool. His throne was flaming with fire, and its wheels were all ablaze. A river of fire was flowing, coming out from before him. Thousands upon thousands attended him; ten thousand times ten thousand stood before him. The court was seated, and the books were opened. Then I continued to watch because of the boastful words the horn was speaking. I kept looking until the beast was slain, and its body destroyed and thrown into the blazing fire. (The other beasts had been stripped of their authority but were allowed to live for a period.)

In my vision at night I looked, and there before me was one like a son of man, coming with the clouds of heaven. He approached the Ancient of Days and was led into his presence.

He was given authority, glory, and sovereign power; all people, nations and men of every language worshipped him. His dominion is an everlasting dominion that will not pass away, and his kingdom his one that will never be destroyed."

THE INTERPRETATION OF DANIEL'S DREAM

In *Daniel 7:15-28* it then goes on to tell us the interpretation of Daniel's dream:

> *"I Daniel, was troubled in my spirit, and the visions that passed through my mind disturbed me. I approached one of those standing there and asked him the true meaning of all this. So, he told me and gave me the interpretation of these things.*
>
> *The four great beasts are four kingdoms that will rise from the earth. But the saints of the Most High will receive the kingdom and will possess it forever – yes, for ever and ever.*
>
> *Then I wanted to know the true meaning of the fourth beast, which was different from all the others and most terrifying, with its iron teeth and bronze claws – the beast that crushed and devoured its victims and trampled underfoot whatever was left. I also wanted to know about the ten horns on his head, and about the other horn that came up, before which three of them fell - the horn that looked more imposing than the others and that had eyes and a mouth that spoke boastfully.*
>
> *As I watched, the horn was waging war against the saints and defeating them, until the Ancient of Days came and pronounced judgement in favour of the saints of the Most High, and the time came that they possessed the kingdom.*
>
> *He gave me this explanation: 'The fourth beast is the fourth kingdom that will appear on earth. It will be different from other kingdoms and will devour the whole earth, trampling it down and crushing it. The ten horns or ten kings that will come from that kingdom. After them another king will arise, different from the earlier ones; he will subdue three kings. He will speak against the Most High and oppress his saints and try to change the set times*

and the laws. The saints will be handed over to him for a time, times and half a time.

But the court will sit, and his power will be taken away and completely destroyed forever. Then the sovereignty, power, and greatness of the kingdoms under the whole heaven will be handed over to the saints, the people of the Most High. His kingdom will be an everlasting kingdom, and all rulers will worship and obey him.'

This is the end of the matter. I, Daniel, was deeply troubled by my thoughts, and my face turned pale, but I kept the matter to myself."

JOHN'S VISION IN REVELATION

We now see the vision that John the Beloved had, with its similarities to the vision given to Daniel, in the book of *Revelation 13:1-9:*

"And I saw a beast coming out of the sea. He had ten horns and seven heads, with ten crowns on his horns, and on each head a blasphemous name. This beast I saw resembled a leopard but had feet like those of a bear and a mouth like that of a lion. The dragon gave the beast his power and his throne and great authority.

One of the heads of the beast seemed to have a fatal wound, but the fatal wound had been healed. The whole world was astonished and followed the beast. Men worshipped the dragon because he had given authority to the beast, and they also worshipped the beast and asked, 'Who is like the beast? Who can wage war against him?'

The beast was given a mouth to utter proud words and blasphemies and to exercise his authority for forty-two months. He opened his mouth to blaspheme God, and to slander his name and his dwelling place and those who live in heaven. He was given the power to make war against the saints and to conquer them. And he was given authority over every tribe, people, language, and nation.

All inhabitants of the earth will worship the beast – all whose names have not been written in the book of life belonging to the Lamb that was slain from the creation of the world. He who has an ear, let him hear.

If anyone is to go into captivity, into captivity he will go.If anyone is to be killed with the sword, with the sword he will be killed. This calls for patient endurance and faithfulness on the part of the saints."

AN INDEPTH LOOK AT THE DREAMS AND VISIONS OF NEBUCHADNEZZAR, DANIEL AND JOHN

Nebuchadnezzar's Dream

Nebuchadnezzar dreamt about a great statue, whose brightness was dazzling, that stood before him and whose form was enormous or awesome in appearance.

Daniel 2: 31-33 stated that the image's head was made of pure gold, his breast and arms were of silver, and his belly, and thighs of bronze; his legs of iron and his feet partly of iron and partly baked clay. A stone that had been cut out without human hands, smashed the image upon his feet that were made of iron and clay, and broke them to pieces.

This is the interpretation of what they both saw:

- The head of gold represents the kingdom of Babylon.
- The silver represents the kingdom of Medes and Persia.
- The bronze represents the kingdom of Greece.
- The iron and clay represent the kingdom of Rome, and divided Rome.

Daniel 2:44 tells us:

> *"In the time of those kings, the God of heaven will set up a kingdom that will never be destroyed, nor will it be left to other people. It will crush all those kingdoms and bring them to an end, but it will itself endure forever. This final kingdom is the kingdom of God, whose kingdom is King Jesus, who is the same God who came to earth as a man. This kingdom shall be victorious over all the kingdoms of earth and will be eternal or never ending."*

Daniel's Dream and Visions

Daniel 7:1 - 7 says that:

> *"Daniel saw the four winds of heaven churning up the great sea. And four great beasts came up from the sea, one different from the other.*
>
> *The first was like a lion; the second was like a bear; the third was like a leopard; and the fourth was terrifying, frightening and very powerful, and had large iron teeth: it crushed and devoured its victims and trampled them underfoot. It was different from all the former beasts, and it had ten horns."*

Here is the interpretation of these four beasts and what they represented:

- The lion represented Babylon from 598 BC – 539 BC
- The bear represents Mede and Persia from 539 BC – 331 BC
- The leopard represents Greece from 331 BC – 168 BC
- The beast with the 10 horns represents Rome, and divided Rome from 168 BC – 538 AD.

This imagery of animals that we see in Daniel confirms and parallels Nebuchadnezzar's dream above, in *Daniel 2:32 – 33.*

THE INTERPRETATION OF THE FIRST BEAST

The first beast was like a Lion and the Lion represents Babylon from 598 BC - 539 BC

God gave king Nebuchadnezzar the right to rule the kingdom of Babylon. He gave him great power, riches, and the rulership over many nations. Nebuchadnezzar, while ruling, had a dream one night as he was lying there and thinking on his bed about what would happen in the future. God then revealed to him what will be in the hereafter.

In his dream, he was shown a great image of a man whose head was of pure gold, whose breast and arm were of silver, and whose belly was of bronze, with his legs of iron, and his feet of iron and baked clay. He was told in his dream that he, Nebuchadnezzar, was the head of gold.

Nebuchadnezzar reigned for thirty-six years in Babylon from 598 BC - 562 BC. During his reign, his heart was lifted up with pride. Because of his pride, he made an image and commanded that everyone within his influence should bow down and worship the image. He dictated that the penalty for not obeying his orders was death, by being thrown into a lake of fire. His heart was so lifted up with pride that he started to believe he was as powerful as God.

Because of his immense pride, God humbled him by letting him eat grass like an animal in the fields and allowed him to be wet with the dew of heaven for seven years. God did this to help show him that he was just a mere man, and not God. After being shown this he came to know who God really is, and he humbled himself and gave honour and praise to the almighty God.

Nebuchadnezzar also then told all those in his kingdom and under his rule to worship the God of heaven, who alone is God. Babylon's wings were also plucked as we know, for Babylon was eventually overthrown by the Medes and Persians in 539 BC *(see Daniel 7:4).*

THE INTERPRETATION OF THE SECOND BEAST

The second beast was like a Bear and the Bear represented Mede and Persia from 539 BC – 331 BC

God then gave Babylon into the hands of the Medes and Persians - all of the kingdom and influence of Babylon. The Medes and the Persians represented the second beast in the dreams and visions of *Daniel 7:5*.

This kingdom was like a bear, and it rose itself upon one side (or lurched from side to side). It was told to, *"Arise and eat a lot of flesh."*

This shows us that out of these two kingdoms, one was going to be much stronger than the other. We see this occurring as the kingdom of the Medes ruled only for two years, while the Persian kingdom ruled for 206 years.

This kingdom was stronger than the Babylonian kingdom because Babylon was now under their control and among all the other territories it captured. The three ribs in the bear's mouth represents Egypt, which is Southward, Libya which is Westward and Babylon which is Northward, which is stated in *Daniel 8:1-7*, which we see below:

> *"In the third year of king Belshazzar's reign, I, Daniel, had a vision, after the one that had already appeared to me. In my vision I saw myself in the citadel of Susa in the province of Elam; in the vision I was beside the Ulai Canal.*

I looked up, and there before me was a ram with two horns, standing beside the canal, and the horns were long. One of the horns was longer than the other but grew up later.

I watched the ram as he charged towards the west and north and south. No animal could stand against him, and none could rescue him from his power. He did as he pleased and became great.

As I was thinking about this, suddenly a goat with a prominent horn between his eyes came from the West, crossing the whole earth without touching the ground.

He came towards the two-horned ram that I have seen standing beside the canal and charged at him in great rage.

I saw him attack the ram furiously, striking the ram and shattering his two horns. The ram was powerless to stand against him; the goat knocked him to the ground and trampled on him, and none could rescue the ram from his power."

The goat we see spoken of here in *Daniel 8:5-7* is speaking of Greece defeating the Medes and Persians. We now come to the time of the third beast, now that the second beast, the Medes and Persians, has been overcome.

THE INTERPRETATION OF THE THIRD BEAST

The third beast was like a Leopard and the Leopard represents Greece from the years 331 BC – 168 BC

The third kingdom was referred to as a leopard, which has the four wings of a bird on its back. The beast also had four heads, and power was given to it.

This beast refers to Greece, who conquered the Medes and Persians under Alexander the Great. He died young, at the age of just thirty-three. While on his deathbed, Alexander was asked who should succeed him, to which he replied, "the strongest". This answer led to his empire being divided into four heads, run by his four generals, Cassander, Ptolemy, Antigonus, and Seleucus (known as the Diadochi or 'successors').

A Brief History of Alexander the Great's Four Generals

This is a brief history of the four generals who succeeded Alexander the Great, during the time of the leopard, the third beast.

1. Cassender (the Greek son of Antipatros also called Antipater, was king of Macedon from 305 BC – 297 BC) He was a king of the ancient kingdom of Macedon from 305 BC – 297 BC and the factor ruler of southern Greece from 317 BC until his death. A son of Antipater and a contemporary of Alexander the Great, Cassender was one of the Diadochi who warred over Alexander's empire following the latter's death in 323 BC. Cassender later seized the crown by having Alexander's son and heir, Alexander IV, murdered. In governing Macedonia from 317 BC – 297 BC, Cassander restored peace and prosperity to the kingdom while founding and restoring numerous cities, (including Thessalonica, Cassandra, and Thebes); however, his restlessness in dealing with political enemies complicates the assessment of his rule.

2. Ptolemy 1 Soter was Pharaoh of Ptolemaic Egypt from 323 BC until his death in 283/282 BC. He was the founder of the Ptolemaic dynasty which ruled Egypt until the death of Cleopatra in 30 BC, turning the country into a Hellenistic kingdom and Alexandria into a centre of Greek culture. The Ptolemaic dynasty, sometimes also known as the Lagid or

Lagdae, was a Macedonian Greek royal family which ruled the Ptolemaic kingdom in Egypt during the Hellenistic period. Their rule lasted for 293 years from 323 BC – 30 BC. They were the last dynasty of ancient Egypt.

3. Antigonus 1(in Ancient Greek, he was also called Antigonus the One-eyed), son of Phillip from Elimaia, was a Macedonian nobleman, general, saptrap and king. He lived from 382 BC - 301 BC. During the first part of his life, he served under Philip 11; after Phillip's death in 336 BC, he served under Phillip's son Alexander the Great.
   He was a major figure in the Wars of Diadochi after Alexander's death, declaring himself king in 306 BC and establishing the Antigonid dynasty. The Antigonid dynasty was a dynasty of Hellenistic kings descended from Alexander the Great's general Antigonos that ruled mainly in Macedonia. The Antigonid dynasty was from 306 – 168 BC.

4. Seleucus 1 Nicator, was born 358 BC and lived until September 281 BC (he was known as one of the Diadochi or 'successors'). He was a Greek general and one of the Diadochi, the rival's general, relative, and friend of Alexander the Great, who fought for control over his empire after his death.
   Having previously served as an infantry general under Alexander the Great, he eventually assumed the title of basileus (king) and established the Seleucid Empire, one of the major powers, of the Hellenistic world, which controlled most of Asia Minor, Syria, Mesopotamia, and the Iranian Plateau until it was overcome by the Roman Republic and Parthian Empire in the late second and early first centuries BC.

THE INTERPRETATION OF THE FOURTH BEAST

Daniel 7:23-26 tells us about the fourth beast. This beast is referring to Pagan Rome. The Roman Kingdom was established in Rome on April 21st, 753 BC and the Roman Republic was established in 509 BC – 27 BC.

During the birth of Christ, Rome was ruled by Emperor Augustus Caesar, who was the first Roman Emperor and reigned from 31 BC to 14 AD.

The Roman Empire was established from 27 BC – 476 AD. In 476 AD Romulus, the last Roman Emperor in the West, who was overthrown by the Germanic leader Odoacer, became the first Barbarian to rule in Rome. The order that the Roman Empire has brought to Western Europe for 1000 years was no more.

The Roman Empire was divided into two parts in 285 AD by Emperor Diocletian, who decided that the Roman Empire was too big to manage. It was divided into two parts, the Eastern Roman Empire, and the Western Roman Empire.

Diocletian was the first Emperor to divide the Roman Empire into a Tetrarchy. In 286 AD he elevated Maximian to the rank of Augustus (Emperor) and gave him control of the Western Empire while he himself ruled East Constantinople.

In 395 AD The Eastern Roman Empire was split again upon the death of Theodosius 1, the Roman Emperor in Constantinople, and was never again to be made whole. He divided the provinces up into east and west between his two sons, Arcadius and Honorius, as it had been under Diocletian's tetrarchy over a century earlier.

The fall of the Eastern Roman Empire or Byzantine Empire in 1453 AD was taken over by The Ottoman Empire.

An empire is a political system in which a group of people are ruled by a single individual, an emperor or empress. The Roman Empire began with the reign of Emperor Augustus. The power of the senate was limited and became an organ to support the emperor.

The period between Augustus and Diocletian is called the High Empire, while the Low Empire is the era between Diocletian and the fall of the Roman Empire in the West. The High Empire was from 31 BC – 305 AD. The Low Empire was from 305 AD – 476 AD.

Ten Western European Nations were formed in 476 AD after the fall of Rome, and they are as follows:

1. Alemanni – Germany
2. Franks – French
3. Burgundians – Switzerland
4. Suevi – Portugal
5. Vandals - The Vandals were a Germanic Tribe that originated in Scandinavia and migrated across Europe.
6. Visigoths – Spain
7. Anglo-Saxons – England
8. Ostrogoths - The Ostrogoths were a Germanic people who established the Ostrogothic Kingdom of Italy, which controlled Italy and neighboring areas from 493 AD to 553 AD.
9. Lombards – Italy
10. Heruli - An east Germanic people originally from Scandinavia.

These nations are the feet (or ten toes) that are spoken of in *Daniel 2:33*, and the ten horns of *Daniel 7: 7*, and the seven heads and ten horns in *Revelation 13:1.*

Iron represented Rome, and Iron mixed with Baked Clay represented divided Rome.

The Beast and the 10 horns in the dreams that Daniel had in *Daniel 7:7 –8* and the visions of John in *Revelation 13:1 - 2*, represent Pagan Rome, and the 10 divided Kingdoms represent the Roman Empire in the West.

Before the time 168 BC until 538 AD in Pagan Rome, the Jews persecuted Christians. During the time of Pagan Rome, Christians tried to escape persecution as best they could by living in caves and mountains. Because Rome was experiencing a lot of infighting, they began to lose control of their Empire. To ensure that they would get back control and the respect of the people, they too started to persecute the Christians, by means of crucifixion, tortures, and imprisonments.

They also made a sport of them by throwing them to the lions in the Colosseum. The emperor found that it was far more exciting for the people to be entertained, as it then took their minds off all the infighting that was happening all around them. It was also easy for them to accomplish this, as they knew that the Christians would not fight back.

In the year 303 AD until 313 AD, persecutions were very rife. Emperor Diocletian, Maximian, Galerius, and Constantius 1 then issued a series of edicts rescinding Christians' legal rights and demanding that they comply with traditional religious practices. Anyone that did not comply and made sacrifices to their gods, was killed. During this period Christians were persecuted by both Jews and Romans.

Emperor Constantine became the emperor of Rome in 306 AD until 337 AD. At the start of his reign the edicts put in place by his predecessors were still in effect, and the Empire was unstable after it had been taken over from Emperor Diocletian, because of the continuous infighting. It was while the kingdom was unstable that Constantine had a dream one night.

In the dream, he dreamt that if he placed the cross before his army as they went into battle, then they would win. He followed the instructions he had heard in his dream and put the cross in front of them as they advanced into battle, and as predicted, they won the battle. Because of their victory, Constantine believed that they had won only because he used the cross of the Christians.

It was from that time on that Emperor Constantine decided to accept that he was a Christian and subsequently commanded everyone in his empire to be called Christians too. This period was called the time of Great Compromising. Although it was a time when Christians were more accepted, it was not without great compromise. Emperor Constantine instructed the Christians to come out of hiding and to worship their God freely in their churches. The Romans were then told, as they too were Christians, to accept the Christians into their churches and to change the names of their gods to the name of the Christian God. Each side was forced to compromise so that he could have a peaceful empire.

It is possible that this was the time when the wheat and weeds were sown in the churches, because true Christians were thrown together with the non-Christians for the sake of the peace of the empire.

Matthew 13:30 tells us:

> *"Let both grow together until the harvest: and in the time of harvest, I will say to the reapers, gather ye together first the weeds, and bind them in bundles to burn them: but gather the wheat into my barn."*

Constantine stood out because he became a Christian and made Jesus the patron of his army. As time has passed, the Christian church and faith grew more organised. In 313 AD, Emperor Constantine and Licinius jointly issued the edict of Milan, which made Christianity a legal religion and officially ended the persecution. Ten years later, Christianity then became the official religion of the Roman Empire.

Pagan Rome came to an end in 538 AD when Emperor Justinian declared himself to be a theologian and no longer a soldier. He then passed on the empire to the church under the leadership of Pope Vigilius. Pagan Rome could not last, as stated in *Daniel 2:40 – 43:*

> *"Finally, there will be a fourth kingdom, strong as iron - for iron breaks and smashes everything – and as iron breaks things to pieces, so it will crush and break all the others.*
>
> *Just as you saw that the feet and toes were partly of baked clay, and partly of iron, so this will be a divided kingdom; yet it will have some of the strength of iron in it, even as you saw iron mixed with clay.*
>
> *As the toes were partly iron and partly clay, so the kingdoms will be partly strong, and partly brittle.*
>
> *And just as you saw, the iron mixed with baked clay, so the people will be a mixture and will not remain united, any more than iron mixes with clay."*

The dragon in *Daniel 7:23 -25* and in *Revelation 13:2*, is Pagan Rome, and this is the dragon that would give his power, seat, and great authority to Papal Rome. In 538 AD until 1798 AD, Papal Rome was ruled by the Popes and the Roman Catholic Church, whose headquarters is the Vatican City in Italy.

Daniel 7:25 says, *"He will speak against the Most High and oppress his saints and try to change the set times and the laws. The saints will be handed over to him for a time, times, and half a time,"* This time, times and half a time represents 3 ½ years.

Revelation 12: 6 says to us, *"The woman fled into the desert to a place prepared for her by God, where she might be taken care of for 1,260 days."* In prophetic terms, remember that a day represents a year. (See confirmation of this in Numbers 14:34; and Ezekiel 4:5-6).

Revelation 13:5 says that the beast was given a mouth to utter proud words and blasphemies; and to exercise his authority for forty-two months, which represents 1260 days (in biblical terms, therefore, 1260 years). The life span of Papal Rome is 1260 years from 538 AD until 1798 AD.

Pagan Rome is the (Dragon) Emperor Justinian, in *Revelation 13:2*, and in *Daniel 7:24* who gave his power to Papal Rome, the (Beast) Pope Vigilius in 538 AD.

This little horn came up among those 10 horns and 3 of those were plucked up by the roots, leaving 7 heads and 10 horns. Those ten kingdoms were now governed by those seven heads, which are as follows:

The Seven Heads

1. Alemanni – Germany
2. Franks – French
3. Burgundians – Switzerland/Sweden
4. Suevi – Portugal
5. Visigoths – Spain

6. Anglo-Saxons – England

7. Lombards – Italy

The other little horn that came up among them that had the eyes of a man, and a mouth uttering proud and blasphemous words, represents Papal Rome, the system and doctrines of the Roman Catholic Church. The Popes are the head rulers.

This was when the role of the state under Emperor Justinian in 538 AD was passed to the church under Pope Vigilius: the Church and State then became one during this time. The Church had the power to act as both Church and State. This powerhouse is called the beast in *Rev 13:2*, who is also the little horn that came up among them in *Daniel 7:24*.

In 533 AD, Emperor Justinian made a decree making John the Bishop of Rome and Chief Bishop of all the churches. The supremacy of the Bishop of Rome over the church could be implemented by Pope Vigilius.

Before 538 AD, the Church dealt only with the affairs of the Church, and the State dealt with the affairs of the State - they were separate. But in 538 AD, the Church was given this power by Emperor Justinian to Pope Vigilius. From then on, the Church had the power to act on behalf of the Church and the State. The Church ruled over all 10 kingdoms, and this came to an end in 1798 AD.

Papal Rome began in 538 AD. Now a new beast was on the scene and a different kind of power emerged. During this time, many Christians were persecuted, murdered, and imprisoned because of their faith. Anyone who would not conform to their doctrines were classed as Heretic. Anyone who was called a Heretic was then punished by imprisonment, beheaded, or burnt at the stake. Crucifixion was banned in the Roman Empire in the 4th century by Emperor Constantine of Rome.

Emperor Constantine 1, on 7th March 321 AD, issued a civil decree making Sunday a day of rest from labour, stating, "All judges and city people and craftsmen shall rest upon the venerable day of the sun."

Sunday Worship Introduced

According to some sources, Sunday worship began when Christians held corporate worship on Sunday in the 1st century. An early example of Christians meeting together on Sunday for the purpose of "breaking bread" and preaching is mentioned in the New Testament book of *Acts 20:7:*

> *"On the first day of the week, we came together to break bread. Paul spoke to the people and, because he intended to leave the next day, kept on talking until midnight."*

In Eastern Christianity, the Sabbath is considered still to be Saturday, the seventh day, in remembrance of the Hebrew Sabbath.

In Catholicism and most sects of Protestantism, the "Lord's Day" is on Sunday, the first day or eighth day.

In Roman culture, Sunday was the day of the sun god. According to paganism, the sun was believed to be a source of life, giving warmth and illumination to mankind. It was the centre of a popular cult among Romans who would stand at dawn to catch the first rays of sunshine as they prayed.

The reason Roman Christianity adopted the number seven, was that they observed seven celestial bodies - the Sun, the Moon, Mercury, Venus, Mars, Jupiter, and Saturn. The Babylonians divided their lunar months into a seven-day week, with the final day of the week holding a particular religious significance.

We started to have 12 months in a year when Julius Caesar's astronomers explained the need for 12 months and the need for the addition of a leap year to synchronise with the season. Some months were both given 30 or 31 days, except for February that has 28 days and 29 days during a leap year, to reflect their importance of being named after Roman leaders.

Three Plucked up by the Roots, which were Subdued

Remember the reference to the three heads being removed? Well, below are the three Kingdoms which were plucked up by the roots in Daniel 7: 8, and the three that were subdued in Rev: 13:24.

The **Vandals** were only in power for a century. They were defeated and many of their leaders killed. Hundreds were conscripted into the Roman army, and others who rebelled were killed. Many of their women married Roman soldiers, and the rest merged into the local population.

The war between the **Ostrogoths** and the Lombards lasted for almost 21 years and caused enormous damage across Italy, reducing the population of the peninsula. Any remaining Ostrogoths in Italy were absorbed into the Lombards, who established a kingdom in Italy in 568 AD.

The **Heruli** kingdom was destroyed by the Lombards in the early 6th century with their last kingdom eventually dominated by Rome, and smaller groups were integrated into larger political entities. The Heruli disappeared from history around the time of the conquest of Italy by the Lombards.

Between 1095 -1492 the Crusades began with attempts by leaders of the three most powerful states of Western Europe. They set out to capture the Holy land following the capture of Jerusalem by Ayyubid

Sultan, an Islamic ruler. Many people lost their lives during those days. The wars were instigated by the Popes and the Church, who were now in charge of the nations' army.

The Church was used to control Western Europe, and all ten nations were ruled by Papal Rome who is the Roman Catholic Church. This was a way to keep the people of Europe as one big family; but the word of God says they will not remain together as iron cannot be mixed with clay.

Henry V111 married Catherine of Aragon in 1509 after the death of his brother Arthur. He later divorced her in 1533 when she was not able to produce a male child for him. This caused a break from the Roman Catholic Church, as they would not agree to him divorcing Catherine.

He told the Church that they should not have departed from the word of God, by allowing him to marry Catherine, as he claimed that the word of God stated that you must not uncover your brother's nakedness. The Roman Catholic Church didn't agree with his wishes though, and so he annulled his marriage with Catherine, so that he could marry again and have an heir to the throne.

He left the Roman Catholic Church and set up another church, called the Church of England, and made himself the head of it. This helped sparked the turning away from the Roman Catholic Church, and other nations also protested, starting the Reformation Period. The Reformation began on the 31st October 1517 until 1648 under Martin Luther, a German monk and theologian, university professor, priest, Father of Protestantism, and church reformer whose ideas started the Protestant Reformation.

Luther taught that salvation is a free gift of God, received only through true faith in Jesus, the Redeemer from sin. Clergy abuses then also caused people to begin criticising the Roman Catholic Church as the greed and scandalous lives of the clergy had created a split between them and the peasants.

The message of Martin Luther's Ninety-Five Theses gave the summary of his beliefs and expressed the same feelings that many of his peers already had about the corruption of Christ's teachings. Luther illustrated the spiritual, material, and psychological truths behind the abuses in the practice of buying and selling indulgences. His followers became known as Protestants and many people and governments adopted the new Protestant ideas put forward by him, while others remained faithful to the Roman Catholic Church. This led to a split in the Church.

As the Church could not keep the 10 nations together as one, this resulted in war, in an effort for control over Europe, and Napoleon Bonaparte who was a French military and political person, became their leader. He rose to prominence during the French Revolution and led several successful campaigns during the Revolutionary Wars.

As Napoleon 1, he was Emperor of the French from 1804 until 1814. His invasion of Russia and Waterloo in Belgium was unsuccessful, and this caused his people to banish him to the Isle of Saint Helena, to prevent him from taking them into any more wars. Therefore, his attempt to keep Europe together as one big family also failed.

Adolf Hitler was an Austrian born German politician who was the dictator of Germany from 1933 to 1945. He rose to power as the leader of the Nazi Party, becoming Chancellor in 1933 and then assuming the title of Fuhrer und Reichskanzier in 1934. He tried to keep Europe together by force, but he was not successful in winning the war for Europe, nor was he able to capture England or keep the unity of the European nations.

THE HISTORY OF SOME OF EUROPE'S KINGS AND QUEENS

Isabella of Aragon from Spain was married to Afonso, Prince of Portugal from 1490 – 1491, and then married Manuel 1 of Portugal in 1497 until August 1498. She died on the 23rd August 1498, and her sister Queen Maria of Aragon married Manuel 1 in the year 1500.

Maximilian 1, an Austrian (a Roman), was married to Anne of Brittany of France from 1490 until 1492 and Bianca Maria Sforza of Italy from 1494 until 1510. Prince Arthur of Wales married Catherine of Aragon from Spain in 1501 and died in 1502 and Catherine went on and married his brother Henry V111, King of England in 1509. She became the Queen of England, but she did not produce a male heir to succeed him, so he divorced her in 1533.

Mary Tudor of England was married to Louis X11 of France from 1514 until 1515, and she also married Charles Brandon, 1st duke of Suffolk and was married to him from 1515 until 1533. She died on the 25th June 1533. King Henry V111 married Anne of Cleves from Dusseldorf, Germany on the 6th January 1540, but the political alliance was no longer to his advantage, so he divorced her on the 9th July 1540.

Amadeo 1 of Spain married Maria Letizia Bonaparte of France, and they were married from 1888 – 1890. Queen Victoria of England was married to Prince Consort, Albert of Saxe-Coburg, Germany from 1840 – 1861, when he died. They had nine children whose spouses were from all over Europe.

Edward V11 married Alexander of Denmark from 1863 until 1910; Victoria Princess Royal married Frederick 111, the German Emperor from 1858 until 1888; Princess Alice of the United Kingdom married Louis 1V, Grand Duke of Neues, from Germany 1862 – 1878; Princess

Beatrice of the United Kingdom married Prince Henry of Battenberg, Germany from 1885 until 1896.

Prince Leopold the Duke of Albany married Princess Helena of Waldeck and Pyrmont, France from 1882 until 1884. Princess Louise, Duchess of Argyll married John Campbell, the 9th Duke of Argyll from 1871 – 1914; Princess Helena of the United Kingdom married Prince Christian of Schleswig-Holstein, Germany from 1866 until 1917;

Alfred, Duke of Saxe-Coburg & Gotha, married the Grand Duchess Maria Alexandrovna of Russia from 1894 until 1900 and Prince Arthur, Duke of Connaught & Strathearn married Princess Louise Margaret of Prussia, Germany in 1879.

We can see as mentioned in *Daniel 2:4 – 43:*

> *"The seeds of men shall try to mingle with each other to keep the power among themselves to become one big family, by not continually fighting each other; but they are not able to cleave to one another even as iron cannot be mixed with clay."*

This speaks of various political attempts to bring nations under one place, but none of those attempts succeeded.

THE EUROPEAN ECONOMIC AND MONETARY SYSTEM BETWEEN THE YEARS 1950 -2020

In 1950 The French Foreign Minister Robert Schuman proposed integrating the Coal and Steel Industries of Western Europe, and in 1951 six countries set up the Coal & Steel Community (ECSC).

In 1957 The Treaties of Rome were signed, creating the European Atomic Energy Community (EURATOM) and the European Economic Community (EEC). The objective of member states is to remove trade and tariff barriers between these countries and to form a Common Market.

In 1957 The Institutions of The Three European Communities (The ECSC, The EEC and the EURATOM) were merged and three new institutions were formed. These three institutions were the European Commission, The Council of Ministers, and The European Parliament.

In 1973 Demark, Ireland and the United Kingdom joined the European Economic Community, and the EEC now has nine member States.

They are -

1. Belgium
2. France
3. Italy
4. Luxembourg
5. Netherlands
6. West Germany
7. Denmark
8. Ireland
9. United Kingdom

In 1979 The Government and Central Banks of the nine member states created the European Monetary System (EMS). Its main feature is the Exchange Rate Mechanism (ERM), which establishes fixed but adjustable exchange rates between the currencies of the participating countries.

- In 1981 Greece joined the European Economic Community.
- In 1986 Spain and Portugal joined the European Community.

- In 1986 The Idea of an Economic and Monetary Union was revived in the Single European Act (SEA).
- In 1988 The European Council confirmed the objective of achieving an Economic and Monetary Union (EMU).
- In 1989 The negotiation of The Treaty on European Union began. This treaty established the European Union (EU) and amended the Treaty that Established the European Community.
- In 1992 The Maastricht Treaty was signed. It introduced new forms of cooperation between member states and governments, for example, the Defense and the Area of Justice and Home Affairs. By adding this

Intergovernmental Cooperation to the existing "Community System," the Maastricht Treaty created the European Union.

- On the 1st November 1993, The Maastricht Treaty came into force after being ratified by all 12 Member States.
- In 1995 Austria, Finland and Sweden joined the European Union.
- Between 1990 – 1999 the Economic & Monetary Union was implemented in three stages.
- In 2002 the euro banknotes and coins were introduced to 12 EU countries.
- On the 1st May 2004 Cyprus, Czech Republic, Estonia, Hungary, Latvia, Lithuania, Malta, Poland, Slovakia, and Slovenia joined the European Union.
- On the 1st December 2009, The Lisbon Treaty came into Force.
- In 2011 three new European Financial Supervisory Authorities came into Operation. They are the European Banking

Authority, the European Insurance & Occupational Pensions Authority, and the European Securities and Markets Authority. They work jointly with the European Systemic Risk Board, which was founded in 2011, to ensure financial stability and improve the EU'S Supervisory Framework.

- On the 1st July 2013 Croatia joined the European Union.
- In 2014 ECB fully assumed supervisory tasks and responsibilities for banks in the member states participating in the Single Supervisory Mechanism.
- In 2020 The United Kingdom withdrew from the European Union.

We can see the fulfilment of Nebuchadnezzar's and Daniel's dreams and visions coming to pass, where the word of God says that they will not remain together, just as iron does not mix with clay. At first it appeared as though countries were united, that there was cooperation between nations, and a sense of unity was going well, but then everything started to split apart.

The United Kingdom was the first nation to come apart from the European Union. It is truly only God who knows how many others will follow and when they will do so.

Daniel 2:42-43 states:

> *"As the toes were partly iron, and partly clay, this kingdom will be partly strong, and partly brittle. And just as you saw iron mixed with baked clay, so the people will be a mixture and will not remain united any more than iron that mixes with clay."*

The ten toes on the feet of the image that Daniel saw in *Daniel 2* and *Daniel 7*, will attempt everything possible in their powers to remain united, but will not be able to do so. For the word of God has made clear that heaven and earth shall pass away, but His words will not pass away, but His word shall accomplish that for which it is sent. His word is true, despite the efforts of man!

At first, the nations referred to as the ten toes under Papal Rome tried to unite Europe by keeping them all as Christian nations in the Roman Catholic Church. This failed, however, when Henry V111 of England broke away and formed the Church of England. Then nations went to war, in an effort to force one another to stick together, but this also failed. Then nations tried by mixing the seeds of men, but this also failed. Last of all, representatives from nations tried to keep them all together by creating the Common Market, to unite the nations and people together economically and politically, but this also is failing.

THE FATAL WOUND OF ONE OF THE HEADS

History also shows us how the prophetic words about the fatal wound of one of the heads came to pass too:

- *Daniel 7:26 says, "But the court will sit, and his power will be taken away and destroyed forever."*
- *Revelation 13:3 says, "One of the heads of the beast seemed to have had a fatal wound, but the fatal wounds had been healed. The whole world was astonished and followed the beast."*
- *Revelation 13:9-10 says, "He who has an ear, let him hear. If anyone is to go into captivity, into captivity he will go. If anyone is to be killed with the sword, with the sword he will be killed. This calls for patient endurance and faithfulness on the part of the saints."*

Between the years 1793 and 1798 during the Reign of Terror, the papacy suffered a great blow, and about 17,000 clergy were killed, and all the lands of the Catholic Church were confiscated and returned into the hands of the state. Also the power of the Church over both State and Church came to an end.

Pope Pius V1 condemned the French Revolution and the suppression of the Gallican Church that resulted from it in 1798, upon the refusal to renounce his temporal power. Pius was taken prisoner and transported to France under the instruction of Napoleon. He then died one year later in Valence. His reign of over two decades is the fourth longest in Papal history.

The beast referred to in scripture is the Roman Catholic Church system. This is the beast that suffered a fatal wound. One of his heads suffered a deadly wound, and its temporal power was abolished by Napoleon Bonaparte, who dissolved the papal state and incorporated Rome, and Latium into his French Empire in 1809.

The Reign of Terror (1793 – 1794) resulted in an estimated 40,000 people being executed or murdered, primarily landed nobility, courtiers, and clergy. A guillotine was set up in the Palace De La Revolution.

The Reign of Terror or simply 'The Terror' was a period of about 11 months during the French Revolution. The French people who did not support the revolution were executed by the guillotine. The Reign of Terror started on 5th September 1793 and ended on the 27th July 1794; over 17,000 clergy had been officially executed, and as many as 10,000 had died in prison or without trial. Historians are estimating that hundreds of thousands more deaths occurred as part of the revolts throughout France or as unrecorded murders, including Louis XV1 and Marie Antoinette.

The positive result of the Reign of Terror was that ordinary people won more political rights and freedoms. The purpose of the Reign of Terror was to purge France of enemies of the Revolution and protect the country from foreign invaders. Robespierre, the head of the Jacobin Club, was removed from power and executed on the 27th July 1794.

Those who perpetrated it justified the Reign of Terror as necessary in bringing democracy to the French People. This was a democracy that had freed the French people from a monarchy that was hoping to destroy the common folk by crushing them with starvation, tensions between the common folk, nobles, and the church.

The revolutionaries further declared that it was the mission and destiny of the French nation to liberate the peoples of Europe from despotism; in other words, to help other peoples of Europe to become nations.

The ideas of the French Revolution were drawn from the period of the Enlightenment, which was influenced by the British political system, inspired by the American Revolution, and shaped by local grievances. The best-known expression of Fresh Revolutionary ideas was the slogan "Liberty, Equality, Fraternity".

Voltaire was a French Enlightenment writer, historian, and philosopher, who attacked the Catholic Church and advocated freedom of religion, freedom of expression, and separation of church and state.

The French Revolution initially began with the attacks on church corruption and the wealth of the higher clergy, an action with which even many Christians could identify, since the Gallican church held a dominant role in pre-revolutionary France.

France provided the money, troops, armament, military leadership, and naval support that tipped the balance of military power in favour of the United States and paved the way for the continental army's ultimate victory, which was sealed at Yorktown, Virginia, five years after Franklin embarked on his mission.

CHANGING SET TIMES AND THE LAWS

Daniel 7:25a says, *"He shall speak against the Most High and oppress his saints and try to change the set times and the laws.*

We can see mention of time, as we were given it by God, by looking at the Bible in Genesis.

Genesis 1:3-5 tells us,

> *"And God said, "Let there be light," and there was light. God saw that the light was good, and he separated the light from the darkness. God called the light "day", and the darkness he called "night". And there was evening, and there was morning - the first day."*

In God's creation, the evening and the morning make up a day. In our time today we can see that this has now been changed by man, because we say in modern times that morning and evening make up a new day. When we are speaking prophetically, for us to understand what is being said, we must use evening and morning just as God designed it.

The enemy has plotted to bring confusion to man by mixing things up - he has also attempted to persuade us as mankind that it is better for us to do as we please and expect God to conform to us, instead of us conforming to the Creator and His way of doing things. If we listen to the way we speak, however, we will see that we still have remnants in our minds of how God planned time, because when it is 12 o'clock at night, we refer to it as midnight, rather than as morning, which is what it is really in God's mind and how He originally designed it.

HEALING OF THE BEAST'S FATAL WOUNDS

The beast's deadly wounds were healed by the signing of the Lateran Treaty. It was signed by Benito Mussolini for the Italian government and by Cardinal Secretary of State, Pietro Gasparri for the papacy and confirmed by the Italian constitution of 1948.

The Lateran Treaty was one component of the Lateran Pacts of 1929, agreements between the Kingdom of Italy under Benito Mussolini and the Holy See under Pope Pius X1 to settle the long standing Roman Question. The treaty and associated pacts were named after the Lateran Palace where they were signed on the 11th February 1929 and ratified by the Italian parliament on the 7th June 1929. The Treaty recognized the Vatican City as an independent state under the sovereignty of the Holy See.

The Italian government also agreed to give the Roman Catholic Church financial compensation for the loss of the Papal States. In 1947, the Lateran Treaty was recognized in the Constitution of Italy as regulating the relations between the state and the Catholic Church.

The papacy was given back the power it once had, to be a state in a state all by itself, and so they were able to govern themselves, and they could defend themselves as a nation.

Popes have more power than kings because they are seen as God's messengers on earth. The Priests, Bishops, and Archbishops all follow the rules of Popes.

Papal supremacy is the doctrine of the Roman Catholic Church - that the Pope by reason of his office as Vicar of Christ and Pastor of the entire Christian Church, has full, supreme, and universal power over the whole Church, a power which he can always exercise unhindered - that in brief the Pope enjoys by Divine Orders.

The Holy See is the last absolute monarchy in the world today. The Pope when he is elected, is answerable to no human powers. He has absolute authority over the entire Roman Catholic Church.

Swiss guards, Italian Guardia Svizzera, Corps of the Swiss soldiers are responsible for the safety of the Pope. They are often called "The world's smallest army". They serve as personal escorts to the pontiff and as watchman for the Vatican City and the Pontifical Villa Castel Gandolfo.

Jesuits are formed by the Society of Jesus which is a religious order of the Catholic Church headquartered in Rome. It was founded by St. Ignatius of Loyola and his six companions with the approval of Pope Paul 111 in 1540. The society is engaged in evangelization and in apostolic ministry in 112 nations.

The Jesuits are an order of Roman Catholic priests. Pope Francis, after his novitiate in the Society of Jesus, Bergoglio, officially became a Jesuit on 12th March 1960, when he made the religious profession of the initial, obedience of a member of the order.

Under St. Ignatius, the Society of Jesus believed that reform in the Catholic Church began with reform of the individual. The founding members of the Society of Jesus took a vow of poverty, chastity, and obedience under Ignatius. Current Jesuits take the same three vows today, along with a vow of obedience to the Pope.

Daniel 2:44 – 45 says,

> *"In the times of those kings, the God of heaven will set up a kingdom that will never be destroyed, nor will it be left to other people. It will crush all those kingdoms and bring them to an end, but it will itself endure forever. This is the meaning of the vision of the rock cut out of a mountain, but not with human hands – a rock that broke the iron, the bronze, the clay, the silver, and the gold to pieces. The great God has shown the king what will take place in the future. The dream is true, and the interpretation is trustworthy."*

We can see that most of the dreams and visions of Nebuchadnezzar, Daniel, and John the revealer have already come to pass. We are now in the time of *Daniel 2: 44-45,* mentioned above, and *Daniel 7:26-27,* when God will put in His appearance. We are told to watch and to be alert, as we don't know the time or the hour before our Lord will come, so let us all be watchful, because what He says to one, he says to all. We are to watch for His coming will be like that of a thief in the night.

CHAPTER 3

THE STUDY OF THE CLEANSING OF THE SANCTUARY

The following is my understanding of the interpretation of the cleansing of the sanctuary in Daniel's vision in the scriptures in *Daniel 8*.

THE BEASTS AND HORNS

Daniel chapter 8:1-17 states:

> *"In the third year of King Belshazzar's reign, I Daniel, had a vision, after the one that already appeared to me. In my vision I saw myself in the citadel of Susa in the province of Elam; In the vision, I was beside the Ulai Canal.*
>
> *I looked up, and there before me was a ram with two horns, standing beside the canal, and the horns were long. One of the horns was longer than the other but grew up later.*
>
> *I watched the ram as he charged towards the west and the north and south. No animal could stand against him, and none could rescue him from his power. He did as he pleased and became great.*

As I was thinking about this, suddenly a goat with a prominent horn between his eyes came from the west, crossing the whole earth without touching the ground.

He came towards the two-horned ram I had seen standing beside the canal and charged at him in great rage.

I saw him attack the ram furiously, striking the ram and shattering his two horns. The ram was powerless to stand against him; the goat knocked him to the ground and trampled on him, and none could rescue the ram from his power.

The goat became very great, but at the height of his power his large horn was broken off, and in its place four prominent horns grew up toward the four winds of heaven.

Out of one of them came another horn, which started small but grew in power to the south, and to the east, and toward the Beautiful Land.

It grew until it reached the host of heaven and it threw some of the starry hosts down to the earth and tramped on them.

It set itself up to be as great as the Prince of the host; it took away the daily sacrifice from him, and the place of his sanctuary was brought low. Because of rebellion, the host of the saints, the daily sacrifice was given over to it. It prospered in everything it did, and truth was thrown to the ground.

Then I heard a holy one speaking, and another holy one said to him, 'How long will it take for the vision to be fulfilled – the vision concerning the daily sacrifice, and rebellion that causes desolation, and the surrender of the sanctuary and of the host that will be trampled underfoot?'

> *He said to me, 'It will take 2,300 evenings and mornings; then the sanctuary will be reconsecrated.'*
>
> *While I, Daniel, was watching the vision and trying to understand it, there before me stood one who looked like a man.*
>
> *And I heard a man's voice from the Ulai calling, 'Gabriel, tell this man the meaning of the vision.'*
>
> *As he came near the place where I was standing, I was terrified and fell prostrate. 'Son of man,' he said to me, 'understand that the vision concerns the time of the end.'"*

This vision that Daniel had is a follow-up to the vision in *Daniel 2:31-45* and *Daniel 7:1-28* where the beasts and horns in his dreams refer to the authorities, powers, and rulers of the kingdom of Babylon, Medes and Persia, Greece, Pagan Rome, and Papal Rome.

This vision was showing Daniel who the successor was who captivated Babylon, the Medes and Persia nations. And it was showing him who "will succeed and captivate them," - Greece, the first Gentile nation to take over that region of the world. It also tells us that when truth is thrown to the ground, the daily sacrifices are taken away, and the sanctuary is brought low.

The starting point of the 2300 days (or in biblical terms, years), prophecy is from 457 BC, in the seventh year of Artaxerxes the king of Persia, who made a decree to Ezra the priest to return to Jerusalem to rebuild the house of the Lord and Jerusalem.

Jerusalem was destroyed by Nebuchadnezzar the Babylonian at that time and the children of Judah and Benjamin were in captivity in Babylon. The 70 weeks prophecy of *Daniel 9*, The 490 years, the time, times and divided of time (3 $^{1/2}$ years) or 42 months, (or 1260 days), are all within that same time- frame: This is because of the biblical principle that in prophetic terms a day is equal to a year (see *Numbers 14:34* and *Ezekiel 4:5-6)*.

The second starting point of the fulfilment of the prophecy in *Daniel 8* is in 538, when Papal Rome began and ended in 1798, after the time when the first Gentile nations captured Persia, and they were captured by the Romans who trampled over God's people for 1260 days, which is 1260 years in prophetic terms.

SOME HISTORY PERTAINING TO ROME

The period between Augustus and Diocletian is called the High Empire, while the Low Empire is the era between Diocletian and the fall of the Roman Empire in the West. The High Empire was from the years 31 BC until 305 AD, and The Low Empire was from 305 AD until 476 AD.

The Ten Western European Nations formed in 476 AD after the dissolution of Rome, and they are as follows:

1. Alemanni – Germany
2. Franks – French
3. Burgundians – Switzerland
4. Suevi – Portugal
5. Vandals - The Vandals were a Germanic Tribe that originated in Scandinavia and migrated across Europe.
6. Visigoths – Spain
7. Anglo-Saxons – England

8. Ostrogoths - The Ostrogoths were a Germanic people who established the Ostrogothic Kingdom of Italy, which controlled Italy and neighboring areas from 493 AD to 553 AD.

9. Lombards – Italy

10. Heruli - The Heruli are an East Germanic people originally from Scandinavia.

These Nations are the feet (or ten toes) of *Daniel 2:33*, and the ten horns of *Daniel 7: 7,* and the seven heads and ten horns referred to in *Revelation 13:1*

<u>The Seven Heads</u>

The Seven Heads are:

1. Alemanni – Germany
2. Franks – French
3. Burgundians – Switzerland/Sweden
4. Suevi – Portugal
5. Visigoths – Spain
6. Anglo-Saxons – England
7. Lombards – Italy

Revelation chapter 11:1-3 states:

> *"I was given a reed like a measuring rod and was told, 'Go and measure the temple of God and the altar and count the worshippers there. But exclude the outer court; do not measure it, because it has been given to the Gentiles. They will trample on the holy city for 42 months. And I will give power to my two witnesses, and they will prophesy for 1260 days, clothed in sackcloth.'*

The 1260 days or (3 ½ years) or 42 months, began in the year 538 and ended in 1798. This is during the time when Papal Rome ruled, and they oversaw both Church and State.

Emperor Justinian passed control over to Pope Vigilius in 538 and the ten Roman kingdoms in the west were now ruled by them.

The three and a half years spoken of in *Daniel 8* refers to the time when the word of God was taken out of the hands of the people and the doctrine now operating in the Roman Catholic church was in full operation. People were told what they should do to inherit eternal life, rather than discovering for themselves what the bible said about being born again.

Access to the bible was removed from the people and was written only in Latin, which is a dead language. Only the Popes were able to understand it, and were allowed and able to deliver the word of God to others. As a result, many false prophets infiltrated the church. The system and doctrines of the Roman Catholic church became predominant and informed people that the way to get to heaven was by their good deeds, not by faith in Jesus. They were also told that they needed to make payment for their dead relatives to be freed out of purgatory and to pay penance in order for their sins to be forgiven. Essentially they were taught that the Pope was given the right to be God here on earth.

THE TWO PROPHETS REMOVED

The two prophets who were removed, referred to in *Revelation 11,* and his two witnesses are the Old and New Testaments, which is the word of God, because these two testaments were taken out of the church, so that no man could read it for themselves to enable them to follow God correctly. Instead, the Pope gave the people direction and guidance on how to worship God, which is unbiblical, but because they considered themselves to be the ultimate authority of God on earth to the people.

True Christians felt very downtrodden during this period of time and fled to live in caves in the mountains, so that they could freely serve the true and living God. Otherwise, the alternative involved them being killed or persecuted. This was the time when Christians were persecuted on a wide scale. Over those 1260 years, thousands and thousands of Christians were killed, by being beheaded, imprisoned, tortured, and being thrown to the lions in the Colosseum.

Between 1793 and 1798 during the Reign of Terror, the papacy then suffered a great blow, and as mentioned, many clergy, about 17,000 clergy were killed, and all the land of the Catholic Church was confiscated and returned into the hands of the state. Also, this was the time when their power as State and Church ended.

Pope Pius V1 condemned the French Revolution and the suppression of the Gallican Church that resulted from it in 1798, upon the refusal to renounce his temporal power. Pius was taken prisoner and transported to France under the instruction of Napoleon. He died one year later in Valence. His reign of over two decades is the fourth longest in Papal history.

The prophecy of the 1290 days and 1335 days is as stated in *Daniel 13:10-12:*

> *"Many shall be purified, and made white, and tried; but the wicked shall do wickedly: and none of the wicked shall understand; but the wise shall understand. And from the time that the daily sacrifice shall be taken away, and the abomination that makes desolate set up, there shall be a thousand two hundred and ninety days. Blessed is he that waited. and cometh to the thousand three hundred and five and thirty days."*

Revelation 11:3-12 states:

> *"And I will give power to my two witnesses, and they will prophesy for 1,260 days, clothed in sackcloth. These are the two olive trees, and two lampstands that stand before the Lord of the earth. If anyone tries to harm them, fire comes from their mouths and devours their enemies. This is how anyone who wants to harm them must die. These men have power to shut up the sky so that it will not rain during the time they are prophesying; and they have power to turn the waters into blood and strike the earth with every kind of plagues as often as they want.*
>
> *Now when they have finished their testimony, the beast that comes up from the Abyss will attack them and overpower and kill them. Their bodies will lie in the street of the great city, which is figuratively called Sodom and Egypt, where also their Lord was crucified.*
>
> *For three and a half days men from every people, tribe, language, and nation will gaze on their bodies and refuse them burial. The inhabitants of the earth will gloat over them and will celebrate by sending each other gifts, because these two prophets had tormented those who live on earth.*
>
> *But after three and a half days a breath of life from God entered them, and they stood on their feet, and terror struck those who saw them.*
>
> *Then they heard a loud voice from heaven saying to them, 'Come up here.' And they went up to heaven in a cloud, while their enemies looked on."*

King Clovis 1 of the Franks was born in 466. He became king when he was just 15 years old in 481 and became the ruler of much of Gaul from 481 to 511. It was a key period during the transformation of the Roman

Empire into Europe. His dynasty, the Merovingians, survived for more than 200 years. Though he was not the first Frankish king, he was the kingdom's political and religious founder.

He got married to Clotilde who was a Catholic Christian in 493, and he converted to Catholicism in 496. On 25 December 508 King Clovis 1 of the Franks got baptised, and he was the first Germanic king to be converted to Catholicism and was considered responsible for spreading Christianity in the Frankish kingdom (France and Germany) and the subsequent birth of the Holy Roman Empire.

The 1290 days vision of *Daniel 12:11* started in 508 when Clovis 1 King of the Franks got baptised, and in 509 King Clovis united all the Frankish tribes under one ruler, changing the form of leadership from a group of petty kings and ended in 1798/1799. This was at the end of the French revolution, which included the last King of France, Louis XV1 and his wife Marie Antoinette, who were both executed for treason by guillotine on the 21 January 1793.

The revolutionaries further declared that it was the mission and destiny of the French nation to liberate the peoples of Europe from despotism - in other words to help other peoples of Europe to become nations.

As stated in *Daniel 12:10-12:*

> *"Many will be purified, made spotless and refined, but the wicked will continue to be wicked. None of the wicked will understand, but those who are wise will understand. From the time that the daily sacrifice is abolished and the abomination that causes desolation is set up, there will be 1290 days.*
>
> *Blessed is the one who waits for and reaches the end of the 1335 days."*

The rejection of religion by the French people started on the 5th October 1793, when the law for a new calendar was passed replacing the seven-day week with a ten-day "decade". Also during this time the months were renamed, and days were allocated differently.

This meant that there was officially no longer a weekly day of worship. This was a major event that initiated the "Dechristianization." Many of the clergy, both Catholic and Protestant, resigned their posts to join the revolution. With excitement being high, the local and regional government proclaimed a grand celebration at the Notre Dame Cathedral.

That was on the 10th November 1793 (or the 20th of Brumaire, according to the new calendar). A Statue of Liberty would replace the image of the "Blessed Virgin." The Mayor of Paris called this ceremony the "Festival of Liberty and Reason."

"The ceremony of the 20th Brumaire" was very important. The insignia of the Catholic religion in the Church of Notre-Dame has been covered up, and a mound has been heaped up, on which stood a Greek Temple, with an inscription – 'To Philosophy' and with four busts of Philosophers. The 'Torch of Truth' was a flame that burned upon an altar. Young girls marched in procession, clad in white, with tricolour sashes, and they wore wreaths of flowers and carried torches in their hands.

Then from the temple there emerged a beautiful woman, dressed in a mantle of blue and wearing a red cap. As the personification of Liberty, she received the homage of the Republicans, who, while stretching their hands towards her, sang a hymn, "Come, holy Liberty, inhabit this temple, become the Goddess of the French People."

This was the time of the worship of reason which was not materialistic or atheistic, but deistic in thought. By this I mean that in peoples' minds they replaced the Creator of Nature with nature itself as the object of worship. Deism thinking was opposed to the doctrine of predestination in which everything that happens is thought to be the will of God, and instead people now tended to believe in the concept of free will, which was developed from Atheism.

THE FRENCH REVOLUTION

The French Revolution had a great and far-reaching impact that transformed the world more than any other revolution. Its repercussions included lessening the importance of religion, the rise of Modern Nationalism, the spread of Liberalism and the igniting of the Age of Revolutions.

Political, social, and economic conditions in France contributed to the discontent felt by many French people - especially those of the third estate. The ideas of intellectuals of the Enlightenment brought new views to government and society.

As mentioned in Chapter 2, the three main goals of the French Revolution were liberty, equality, and fraternity. Liberty meant that everyone had all their natural rights and freedoms. Equality meant that everyone would be equal in the eyes of the government. Fraternity meant that everyone would get along and respect each other's rights.

The positive result of the Reign of Terror is that ordinary people won more political rights and freedoms. The purpose of the Reign of Terror was to purge France of its enemies of the Revolution and protect the country from foreign invaders. Robespierre, the head of the Jacobin Club, was removed from power and executed on the 27th July 1794.

On the 21st January 1793 until the 10th June 1796, three and half days represented three and half years, as stated in *Revelation 11:3-12.*

During the Reign of Terror the French nation de-Christianized the church and changed the time of the week to a 10-day week.

This was the fulfilment of the word of God which came to pass as stated in *Daniel 8:11-13:*

> *"It set itself up to be as great as the prince of the host; it took away the daily sacrifice from him, and the place of his sanctuary was brought low.*
>
> *Because of rebellion the host of the saints and the daily sacrifice was given over to it. It prospered in everything it did, and truth was thrown to the ground.*
>
> *Then I heard a holy one speaking, and another holy one said to him, 'How long will it take for the vision to be fulfilled – the vision concerning the daily sacrifice, the rebellion that causes desolation, and the surrender of the sanctuary and of the host that will be trampled underfoot?'*
>
> *He said to me, 'It will take 2,300 evenings and mornings; then the sanctuary will be reconsecrated.'"*

The nation of France was under Napoleon their general during this time. Through him the daily sacrifice was taken away, and the place of God's sanctuary was thrown out. A host was given to him against the daily sacrifice by the reason of rebellion, and truth was trampled to the ground, and it practised, and prospered. During these three and a half years anyone who would be found with the bible or anything to do with Christianity would be killed by the guillotine. Because the word of God was thrown out, people's hearts became more evil, and wickedness increased, including the elimination of all who professed to be Christians from their nation.

The first King of France, Clovis 1, was baptised on the 25th December 508 and united the European nation politically. He also Christianized all of Europe, and the last King of France, Louis XV1 was beheaded along with his wife Marie Antoinette during the Reign of Terror on 21 January 1793. During the time when France became De-Christianized in 1798/99, France was no longer ruled by monarchies, and they became a Republic State.

The French Revolution was a period of radical political and social change in France that began with the Estates Generals in 1789 and ended with the formation of the French Consulate in November 1799.

The start of the 70 weeks prophecy in *Daniel 9:24-27* was around the year 457 BC and ended around 36 AD after the ascension of Jesus into heaven and the stoning of Steven. *(see Act 7:54-60)*.

The periods of time referred to in different ways, such as time, times and divided of times, three and half years, the forty-two months and one thousand two hundred and threescore days are all talking about the same timeframe. This started in 538 and ended in 1798, the starting and ending of Papal Rome. A day represents a year in prophetic terms as we know, so it was a period of 1,260 years. *(see Numbers 14.34 and Ezekiel 4:5-6):*

The prophecy of the 1290 days and 1335 days stated in *Daniel 13:10-12* began in 508 when King Clovis 1 was baptised and then Christianised the European nations and it ended in 1798/9 during the Reign of Terror when the nation of France was de-Christianized. The nation had thrown out God during this time as well as the Bible and killed all Christians and anyone who was found with the Bible or anything to do with Christianity, and also got rid of the last King of France, Louis XV1.

We see all of this stated in *Daniel 12:12:*

> *"Blessed is the one who waits for and reaches the end of the 1335 days."*

This then brings us to the time of 1843 when it is stated that the sanctuary will be cleansed. By this time the Bible was reintroduced back into churches, and written not just in Latin but in the language of the people. The printing press was now in full operation and because of it, the printing of vast numbers of books was now available, making it affordable to even the common folk.

The Bible was produced in bulk in many different languages and spread all over the world. In our modern world today we can obtain the word of God easily and read it on many different media devices, even on our phones, enabling most of the world's people today to have access to the word of God.

The word of God states that blessed is the one who waits for and reaches the end of the 1,335 day. This period referred to here began in the year 1843 when people stopped fleeing from these ten European nations because of the persecutions and killings or imprisonment for the words of God and for practising Christianity and worshipping God.

People from that time on from the regions of those Ten Horns were then free to worship God as they so wished. This included the period from 1843 to our present time and to the return of Jesus our Saviour and Redeemer.

Daniel 2:34-35 states:

> *"While I was watching, a rock was cut out, but not by human hands. It struck the statue on his feet of iron and clay and smashed them.*

Then the iron, the clay, the bronze, the silver, and the gold were broken to pieces at the same time and became like the chaff on threshing-floors in the summer. The wind swept them away without leaving a trace. But the rock that struck the statue became a huge mountain and filled the whole earth."

Daniel 7: 9-11 & 12-18 then states:

"As I looked, thrones were set in place, and the Ancient of days took his seat. His clothing was white as snow; the hair of his head was white like wool. His thrones were flaming with the fire, and its wheels were all ablaze.

A river of fire was flowing, coming out from before him. Thousands upon thousands attended him: ten thousand times ten thousand stood before him. The court was seated, and the books were opened.

Then I continued to watch because of the boastful words the horn was speaking. I kept looking until the beast was slain, and its body destroyed and thrown into the blazing fire.

In my vision at night I looked and there before me was one like a son of man, coming with the clouds of heaven. He approached the Ancient of Days and was led into his presence.

He was given authority, glory, and sovereign power; all people, nations and men of every language worshipped him. His dominion is an everlasting dominion that will not pass away, and his kingdom is one that will never be destroyed.

I, Daniel, was troubled in my spirit, and the visions that passed through my mind disturbed me. I approached one of those standing there and asked him the true meaning of all this.

So, he told me and gave me the interpretation of these things:

'The four great beasts are four kingdoms that will rise from the earth.

But the saints of the Most High will receive the kingdom and possess it forever - yes forever and ever.'

The word of God is telling us about the time when Jesus will return and fight for His saints. He will give the kingdom to the saints to possess it forever. It will be during the reign of these four kingdoms on earth. The kingdom that will be given to the saints is the 'New Jerusalem which came down from heaven.' When Jesus returns and judges the unrighteous, they will be punished and their punishment is the second death, which is total separation from God.

THE SANCTUARY OF GOD

We shall be looking in detail at the sanctuary, and the 2300 days when the sanctuary shall be reconsecrated.

The sanctuary story is all about the great love of God for humanity and His salvation plan to restore man back to Himself.

Exodus 25:1-40 states:

"The Lord said to Moses, 'Tell the Israelites to bring me an offering. You are to receive the offering for me from each man whose heart prompts him to give.

These are the offerings you are to receive from them: gold, silver, and bronze, blue, purple, scarlet yarn, and fine linen; goat hair, ram skins dyed red and hides of sea cows, acacia wood. Olive oil for the light; spices for the anointing oil and the fragrant incense.

And onyx stones and other gems to be mounted on the ephod and breast piece.

Then have them make a sanctuary for me, and I will dwell among them. Make this tabernacle and all its furnishing exactly like the pattern I will show you. Have them Make a chest of acacia wood - two and a half cubit long, a cubit and a half high.

Overlay it with pure gold, both inside and out, and make a gold mounting around it. Cast four gold rings for it and fasten them to its four feet, with two rings on one side and two rings in the other. Then make poles of acacia wood and overlay them with gold. Insert the poles into the rings on the sides of the chest to carry it. The poles are to remain in the rings of this ark: they are not to be removed. Then put in the ark the testimony, which I will give you.

Make an atonement cover of pure gold – two and a half cubits long and a cubit and a half wide. And make two cherubim out of hammered gold at the ends of the cover. Make one cherub on one end and the second cherub on the other: make the cherubim of one piece with the cover, at the two ends.

The cherubim are to have their wings spread upwards, overshadowing the cover with them. The cherubim are to face each other, looking toward the cover. Place the cover on top of the ark and put in the ark the testimony, which I will give you.

There, above the cover between the two cherubims that are over the ark of the testimony, I will meet with you and give you all my commands for the Israelites. Make a table of acacia wood - two cubits long, a cubit wide and a cubit and a half high. Overlay it with pure gold and make a gold moulding round it.

Also make around it a rim a handbreadth wide and put a gold moulding on the rim. Make four gold rings for the table and fasten them to the four corners, where the four legs are.

The rings are to be close to the rim to hold the poles used in carrying the table.

Make the poles of acacia wood, overlay them with gold and carry the table with them.

And make its plates and dishes of pure gold, as well as the pitchers and bowls for the pouring out of the offering. Put the bread of the Presence on this table, to always be before me.

Make a lampstand of pure gold and hammer it out, base and shaft; its flower-like cups, buds and blossoms shall be of one piece with it. Six branches are to extend from the sides of the lampstand - three on one side and three on the other.

Three cups shaped like almond flowers with buds and blossoms are to be on one branch, three on the next branch, and the same for all six branches extending from the lampstand.

And on the lampstand, there are to be four cups shaped like almond flowers with buds and blossoms. One bud shall be under the first pair of branches extending from the lampstand, a second bud under the second pair, and a third bud under the third pair - six branches in all.

The buds and branches shall all be of one piece with the lampstand, hammered out of pure gold. Then make its seven lamps and set them up on it so that they light the space in front of it. Its wick trimmers and trays are made of pure gold.

> *A talent of pure gold is to be used for the lampstand and all these accessories.*
>
> *See that you make them according to the pattern shown on the mountain.'"*

We will see that everything in the sanctuary represents Jesus Christ our Redeemer.

Psalms 77:13 states:

> *"Thy way, O God, is in the sanctuary: who is as great a God as our God?"*

To enter the sanctuary the children of Israel would need to enter it by the Eastern Gate, because then the children of Israel would always have their backs towards the sun, making it clear to them that they serve the Living God the Creator, and are not to worship the created things such as the Sun, the Moon, the stars or any other part of creation.

As we enter the sanctuary we come into the outer court where we come first to the brazen altar *(see Exodus 27:1-8)*. This is where the children of Israel would take their sacrificial offering to the priest and confess their sins. The priest would then record their sins and transfer those sins to the sacrificial animal.

This animal was required to be without blemish, and could be a bull, or a lamb, or a goat, or pigeon depending on how wealthy or poor the people were. The priest would then collect some of the blood from the animal that was killed for the sacrifice.

This is the first action that our Lord and Saviour took on our behalf in the wonderful plan of redemption. Jesus is our sanctuary and our sacrificial Lamb, and when we come to Him, we confess our sins, and

He forgives us and covers us with His blood. *(See Exodus 25:8-9, John 1:29 & John 1:36).*

Exodus 25:8-9 says:

> *"And let them make me a sanctuary, that I may dwell among them. According to all that I show thee, after the pattern of the tabernacle, and the pattern of all the instruments thereof, even so shall ye make it."*

John 1:29 says,

> *"The next day John seeth Jesus coming unto him, and saith, 'Behold the Lamb of God, which taketh away the sin of the world.'"*

In *John 1:36* we see,

> *"And looking upon Jesus as he walked, he said, 'Behold the Lamb of God!'*

We then come to the laver of water where the priest would wash his hands and feet to enable him to take the sacrificial blood into the tabernacle. This represents part of what God has made available for us as His children.

After we confess our sins to God, our next step is to go through water baptism, a cleansing that gives us spiritual life and protects the believer from the uncleanness of the world, showing the world that we have accepted Jesus as our Saviour. Through the act of water baptism, we have publicly confessed that we are now dead to sin and alive to righteousness, and that we are now followers of Christ and walk in the righteousness of Jesus, and not in our own righteousness.

After the laver, we then came to the tabernacle, where only priests were allowed to go. They were required to enter it when they were clean only, and to take the sacrificial blood of the children of Israel and to apply that blood on the altar of incense.

This is symbolic of what Jesus is to us - Jesus is our tabernacle or temple as stated in *Revelation 21:22*, which says, *"I did not see a temple in the city, because the Lord God Almighty and the Lamb are its temple."*

The temple in the city referred to here in Revelation is speaking of the new Jerusalem in heaven, when we will finally live with Christ in the new heaven. However, right here on earth also, our bodies are the temple or tabernacle of the Holy Spirit, where we commune with God in our spirits. Jesus is our sacrificial Lamb and He has already acted as our High Priest and has taken His blood, once and forever, to the Father for our Redemption.

When we enter the tabernacle we see that there are three items in there, and they are the table of shewbread, the candlestick, and the altar of incense.

John 6:35 states that,

> *"Then Jesus declared, 'I am the bread of life. He who comes to me will never go hungry, and he who believes in me will never be thirsty.'"*

The shewbread in the sanctuary represents Jesus who is our bread of life. When we come to Christ and confess our sins and begin to follow Him, for us to survive, and continue to grow as Christians, we need to eat the bread of life. It is literally food for our spirit man. The bread spoken of here is the word of God. Because we do not know how to walk holy before a Holy God without guidance, the word of God is there to guide us on the right path to enable us to walk in His righteousness.

If we do not read the words of God daily for guidance we won't grow spiritually, and we will remain like babies requiring milk instead of solid food.

We see this in *1 Corinthians 3:1-3* which says,

> *"Brothers, I could not address you as spiritual, but as worldly – mere infants in Christ. I give you milk, not solid food, for you were not yet ready for it. Indeed, you are still not ready. You are still worldly. For since there is jealousy and quarrelling among you, are you not worldly? Are you not acting like mere men?"*

The candlestick also represents Jesus. He is the light of the world, and if we do not come to the light we will forever be living in darkness. Anyone walking in darkness will stumble.

For us to grow we need to go into the tabernacle where the shewbread and the candlestick are, where there is spiritual food for us to eat, and where the light can guide us to see where to go and what to do, to enable us to live a holy life.

The third item in the holy place in the tabernacle is the altar of incense, and this is the place where the priest takes the sacrificial blood of the animal and puts some of the blood on the tip of the horn on the altar and then sprinkles the rest of the blood at the base of the altar. The priest also burns sweet smelling incense on the altar.

This is symbolic again of Jesus. Jesus is our Intercessor and our High Priest, and Jesus intercedes for us to the Father. As our Intercessor, He is literally our go-between between us and the Father. When we come to God in prayer and let our petitions be known to Him, our prayer is ascended as a sweet-smelling savour to God. It is a pleasant smell to Him!

Hebrews 4:14-16 states:

> *"Therefore, since we have a great High Priest who has gone through the heavens, Jesus the Son of God, let us hold firmly to the faith we profess. For we do not have a High Priest who is unable to sympathise with our weaknesses, but we have one who has been tempted in every way, just as we are - yet was without sin. Let us then approach the throne of grace with confidence, so that we may receive mercy and find grace to help us in our time of need."*

Next, we then come through the veil into the Holy of Holies, which contains just one item, the ark of the covenant. On top of the ark is the mercy seat and the cherubim, and inside of the ark are the two tablets of the testimonies, the Ten Commandments, Aaron's rod that budded and the Manna.

The High Priest was the only person who could enter the Holy of Holies, which he would enter just once a year, on the day of atonement. This is when the high priest would sacrifice a bullock for the sins of himself and the sins of his family. He was not permitted to enter the Holy of Holies unclean, for if he entered with sin in his life he would die.

The High Priest would cleanse himself and the children of Israel, by taking the blood of the sin offerings into the Holy of Holies and sprinkle the blood over the mercy seat for the atonement of their sins. Only then would the sins of the people be forgiven fully, and this would take place once a year, and the year would then start all over again.

At the death, burial and resurrection of Jesus Christ, Jesus became our sacrificial Lamb and High Priest. He has taken His blood to the sanctuary in Heaven and He presented it to the Father on the mercy seat where the ark of the covenant stands, for the full atonement of the sins of Humanity, once and for all.

This never needs to be done again and so there is no more need for us to revert to animal sacrifices for our sin, nor is it only covered for one year. Our sins are forgiven, past, present and future by that one act of Jesus.

Jesus is our High Priest now in the sanctuary in heaven, in the Holy of Holies atoning for us. The prophecy of *Daniel 8:13-14* speaks of this time and it says:

> *"Then I heard a holy one speaking, and another holy one said to him, 'How long will it take for the vision to be fulfilled – the vision concerning the daily sacrifice, the rebellion that causes desolation, and the surrender of the sanctuary host that will be trampled underfoot?'*
>
> *He said to me, 'It will take 2,300 evenings and mornings; then the sanctuary will be reconsecrated.'"*

This prophecy was speaking of the time when the sanctuary would be cleansed - and reconsecrated to God. No longer would there be a daily sacrifice. According to this vision of *Daniel 8,* the time for the cleansing of the sanctuary is from the year 1743/4. The word of God says blessed are those who come to the one thousand three hundred and thirty-five days. This is when the sanctuary would be cleansed completely.

The vision here is talking about the heavenly sanctuary, and we can see through history that the earthly sanctuary was destroyed in 70 AD after the ascension of Jesus into heaven. The earthly sanctuary was cleansed once a year on the day of atonement when the High Priest would enter the Holy of Holies, carrying the sin offering of the sacrificial goat to sprinkle on the mercy seat.

Our High Priest Jesus Christ has taken on this role, as He was found worthy to present His blood to the Father. Jesus is now our High Priest and has been carrying out judgement in the heavenlies with God the Father and the angels. There is no longer a need for the once yearly cleansing of the earthly sanctuary!

When Jesus returns, He will already know who belongs to Him, because our names would have been written in the Lamb's book of life, and we would be sealed by his angels.

1 Peter 4:17-19 says to us:

> *"For it is time for judgement to begin with the family of God; and if it begins with us, what will the outcome be for those who do not obey the gospel of God?*
>
> *And 'If it is hard for the righteous to be saved, what will become of the ungodly and sinner?'*
>
> *So then, those who suffer according to God's should commit themselves to their faithful Creator and continue to do good."*

Since the fulfilment of the prophecy in *Daniel 8, 9 and 12,* we have now entered the last days, and yet no man knows when Jesus shall return, but the word of God states that it will be in the last days. He also says that He will not give his kingdom to another. At the end of the fulfilment, the time period of those four beasts, He will be setting up His kingdom and His holy ones will possess the kingdoms for ever and ever.

Daniel 7: 9-11 & 12-18 states:

> *"As I looked, thrones were set in place, and the Ancient of days took his seat. His clothing was as white as snow; the hair of his head was white like wool. His throne was flaming with fire, and its wheels were all ablaze.*

A river of fire was flowing, coming out from before him. Thousands upon thousands attended him; ten thousand times ten thousand stood before him. The court was seated, and the books were opened.

Then I continued to watch because of the boastful words the horn was speaking. I kept looking until the beast was slain, and his body destroyed and thrown into the blazing fire. The other beasts had been stripped of their authority but were allowed to live for a period.

In my vision at night I looked, and there before me was one like a son of man, coming with the clouds of heaven. He approached the Ancient of days and was led into his presence.

He was given authority, glory, and sovereign power; all peoples, nations and men of every language worshipped him. His dominion is an everlasting dominion that will not pass away, and his kingdom is one that will never be destroyed.

I Daniel, was troubled in my spirit, and the visions that passed through my mind disturbed me. I approached one of those standing there and asked him the meaning of all this. So, he told me and gave me the interpretation of these things:

'The four great beasts are four kingdoms that will rise from the earth.

But the saints of the Most High will receive the kingdom and possess it forever, even forever – yes, and forever and ever.'"

The prophecy clearly tells us that there will be a time of four kingdoms ruling - referred to as the four beasts, the nations of which were explained earlier, and then after that will come the time of the kingdom of God - under the rulership of Jesus. And we His saints will rule with Him in His kingdom!

CHAPTER 4

THE STUDY OF THE BOOK OF MATTHEW CHAPTER 24

The following is my understanding of the Interpretation of Jesus' answers to the three questions his disciples asked him in *Matthew Chapter 24:3,* which are:

1. **"Tell us," They said, "when will this happen?**
2. **And what shall be the sign of your coming?**
3. **And what of the end of the age?"**

They were asking these three questions because they are related to the Last Days and His disciples didn't fully understand what Jesus was saying to them.

I will be looking at the three questions the disciples asked Jesus on the Mount of Olives *(see Matthew 24:1-3)* and attempt to give my understanding of them.

These questions are related specifically to Jesus' response after He and the disciples departed the temple and the disciples drew His attention to its buildings.

"Jesus answered them, 'Do you see all these things? Truly I tell you, not one stone here will be left on another, everything will be thrown down.'" (Matthew 24:2).

We see in *Matthew 24:4-21* again how Jesus answered them to let them know what was going to occur:

"Jesus answered, 'Watch out that no one deceives you. For many will come in my name, claiming, 'I am Christ,' and will deceive many. You will hear of wars and rumours of wars but see to it that you are not alarmed. Such things must happen, but the end is still to come. Nation shall rise against nation, and kingdom against kingdom. There will be famines and earthquakes in various places. All these are the beginning of birth pains.

Then you will be handed over to be persecuted and put to death, and you will be hated by all nations because of me. At that time many will turn away from the faith and will betray and hate each other. And many false prophets will appear and deceive many people. Because of the increase of wickedness, the love of most will grow cold.

But he who stands firm to the end, will be saved. And this gospel of the kingdom will be preached in the whole world as a testimony to all nations, and then the end will come.

So, when you see standing in the holy place 'the abomination that causes desolation,' spoken of through the prophet Daniel let the reader understand -then let those who are in Judaea flee to the mountains. Let no-one on the root of the house go down to take anything out of the house. Let no-one in the field go back to take his cloak. How dreadful it will be in those days for pregnant women and nursing mothers! Pray that your flight will not take place in winter or on the sabbath. For then they will be in great distress, unequalled from the beginning of the world until now – and never to be equaled again."

I shall start my explanation from verse 15-21:

David, during the time of his reign as king of Israel, had it in his heart to build a temple for the name of the Lord, the God of Israel, but the LORD said to David, *"Because it was in your heart to build a temple for my name, you did well to have this in your heart. Nevertheless, you are not the one to build the temple, but your son, who is your own flesh and blood – he is the one who will build the temple unto my Name." (2 Chronicles 6:8-9).*

We can see that the Lord has not asked David to build him a temple. It was David who wanted to build the Lord a temple out of his own heart's desire. The Lord asked David to be king over his people Israel though - He did not ask him to build a temple. The Lord instructed Moses on how to build the tabernacle of the Lord, for the children of Israel; they were to take the tabernacle wherever they went. It was not meant to be a building that cannot be moved; they were to carry the tabernacle as a tent with them.

The tabernacle held the Ark of the Covenant and all the holy vessels. Moses was instructed by God exactly how to build the tabernacle, and it was to be built exactly as the tabernacle was in heaven.

The Lord accepted what David wanted, but it was not what God wanted, just as when God went along with the children of Israel wanting a king. Even though sometimes God may allow us to do things we want to do, it is not always His full will and desire. God was the One who was Israel's King, but the children of Israel demanded a king like the other nations, and so God gave them their desires. They did not accept God's plans for Him to be their king, for they rejected Him and wanted their own king to rule them.

1 Kings 8 tells us about when the first temple was built by king Solomon, the son of king David. He dedicated the temple and blessed all the congregation of Israel and prayed to God for the forgiveness of His people. Solomon promised God that if they sinned and committed any wickedness, and then returned and asked for forgiveness, that God would hear from His temple and forgive them their trespasses.

In Deuteronomy 28, Moses told the children of Israel to observe and do all the commandments of God, which he commanded them to do. They were told then that if they obeyed the voice of the Lord their God, then they would be blessed. The Lord would set them high above all the nations of the earth: and all the blessings mentioned in *Deuteronomy 28:3-14* would be theirs to have, and they would not have need of anything. But if they didn't obey, then all the curses in *Deuteronomy 28:15-68* would come upon them until they were destroyed.

After the death of King Solomon, the children of Israel were split into two groups, the Northern and the Southern tribes. One tribe would be that of **Judah and Benjamin**, and the other tribe, that of **Israel**. The tribe of **Judah and Benjamin were called Jews**, and the **tribe of Israel were called Samaritans.**

Both tribes did evil in the sight of God and did not obey the commandments and statutes of God. Because of their disobediences, both tribes were put into captivity. Judah and Benjamin were put in captivity in Babylon, and Israel was put in captivity in Assyria.

The first temple that was built by King Solomon was destroyed. On the 17th May 586 BC by Nebuzaradan, *2 Kings 25:8-17* refers to this and it states:

> *"On the seventh day of the fifth month, in the nineteenth year of King Nebuchadnezzar king of Babylon, Nebuzaradan commander of the imperial guard, an official of the king of Babylon, came to Jerusalem. He set fire to the temple of the Lord, the royal palace*

> *and all the houses of Jerusalem. Every important building, he burned down. The whole Babylonian army, under the commander of the imperial guard, broke down the walls around Jerusalem.*
>
> *Nebuzaradan, the commander of the guard, carried into exile the people who remained in the city, along with the rest of the populace and those who had gone over to the king of Babylon. But the commander left some of the poorest people of the land to work in the vineyards and fields.*
>
> *The Babylonians broke up the bronze pillars, the moveable stands and the bronze sea that were at the temple of the Lord, and they carried the bronze to Babylon. They also took away the pots, shovels, wick trimmers, dishes and all the bronze articles used in the temple service. The commander of the imperial guard took away the sensors and sprinkled bowls – all that was made of pure gold or silver.*
>
> *The bronze from the two pillars, the sea and the moveable stands, which Solomon had made for the temple of the Lord, was more than could be weighted. Each pillar was twenty-seven feet high, the bronze capital on top of the pillar was four and a half feet high and was decorated with a network and pomegranates of bronze all around. The other pillar, with its network, was similar."*

Years later, Daniel made supplication to God on behalf of his people, the children of Judah and Benjamin. He saw by their behaviour that they were still walking in the way of the curses and not the blessings while they were in captivity in Babylon.

Daniel 9:11 states,

> *"All Israel has transgressed your law, and turned away, refusing to obey you. Therefore, the curses and sworn judgements written in*

the law of Moses, the servant of God, have been poured out on us, because we have sinned against you."

The people of Judah and Benjamin were nearing the time of their 70 years captivity in Babylon and the desolation of Jerusalem. Daniel prayed and asked God for forgiveness for the sins of himself and his people. He saw that the time to return to Jerusalem was fast approaching, but his people were not obeying God's commandments or statues. *(Daniel 9:1-14).*

THE FIRST QUESTION: "WHEN WILL THIS OCCUR?"

We see that despite the people still not obeying God, God the Merciful One told Daniel that He was still giving his people a chance to end their sins.

Daniel 9:24-27 declares:

"Seventy 'sevens,' are decreed for your people your holy city, to finish the transgression, to put an end to sin, to atone for wickedness, to bring in everlasting righteousness, to seal up vision and prophecy and to anoint the Most Holy Place.

Verse 24 above shows us that God was still giving His people another Seventy sevens in days (or years) to have time to stop sinning.

It continues with *verses 25-27:*

"Know and understand this: From the time the word goes out to restore and rebuild Jerusalem until the Anointed One, the ruler, comes, there will be seven 'seven', and sixty-two 'sevens.' It will be re-built with streets and a trench, but in a time of trouble.

After sixty-nine 'sevens', the Anointed One will be put to death and will have nothing. The people of the ruler who will come will destroy the city and the sanctuary. The end will come like a flood: War will continue until the end, and desolation has been decreed.

He will confirm a covenant with many for one 'seven'. In the middle of the 'seven' He will put an end to sacrifice and offering. And at the temple, he will set up an abomination that causes desolation, until the end that is decreed is poured out on him."

After the return of the children of Judah and Benjamin from the captivity of Babylon, they were given the chance to go and rebuild the temple, the city, and the walls of Jerusalem, by Cyrus, Darius, and Artaxerxes the kings of Persia. Babylon was eventually overthrown by the king of the Medes and Persians.

During this time, the children of Judah and Benjamin were having a lot of trouble from their brethren, the other ten tribes, the children of Israel. They were preventing them from rebuilding the temple, the city, and the walls of Jerusalem. But despite their intervention, the children of Judah and Benjamin were still able to rebuild the temple, the city and walls, as God informed Daniel in a vision *(see Daniel 9)*. It was this same temple which the disciples drew Jesus' attention to, when He replied that there would not be one stone left upon another which shall not be thrown down *(see Matthew 24:2)*.

The children of Judah and Benjamin were given seventy 'sevens', which in prophetic terms equaled 70 x 7 weeks, or a total of 490 days, each day then representing one year. *(Numbers 14:34* reads, *for forty years – one year for each of the forty days you explored the land - you will suffer for your sins and know what it is like to have me against you).*

They were given this number of years to finish the transgressions, in other words to stop sinning, and not only to make an end of their sins, but also to make reconciliation for their iniquity, and to bring in everlasting righteousness, to seal up vision and prophecy, and to anoint the Most Holy *(see Daniel 9:24).*

During the time of Jesus' ministry, the children of Judah and Benjamin were still following in the ways that would result in the curse being poured out upon them. They still did not obey the voice of the Lord their God, or walk in his ways, and they rejected Jesus the Anointed One by crucifying Him, which brought the wrath of God upon them. However, even still, we know that on the cross, Jesus took the wrath of God for all people *(see Isaiah 53 which tells us how He carried the punishment for all transgressions for all people.)*

Luke 19:37-46 reads:

> *"When he came near the place where the road goes down the mount of Olives, the whole crowd of disciples began joyfully to praise God in loud voices for all the miracles they had seen.*
>
> *'Blessed, is the King who comes in the name of the Lord! Peace in heaven and glory in the highest!'*
>
> *Some of the Pharisees in the crowd said to Jesus, 'Teacher, rebuke your disciples.'*
>
> *'I tell you,' He replied, 'if they keep quiet, the stones will cry out.'*
>
> *As he approached Jerusalem and saw the city, he wept over it, and said, 'If you, even you, had only known on this day what would bring you peace – but now it is hidden from your eyes. The days will come upon you when your enemies build an embankment against you and encircle you and hem you in on every side. They will dash you to the ground, you the children within your walls. They will not leave one stone on another, because you did not recognize the time of God's coming to you.'*

> *Then he entered the temple area and began driving out those who were selling.*
>
> *'It is written,' he said to them, 'My house will be a house of prayer', but you have made it a den of robbers.'"*

We can see, although they loved to draw attention to the beauty of the temple, they did not have respect for it as a place of worship. Their hearts were far from reverencing God. The temple had become an object to boast about, instead of being used for the purpose for which it was built.

The main reason for the tabernacle was for the children of Israel to carry it around with them, just as we are now the tabernacle of God, carrying the Holy Spirit within us. Jesus was not really very concerned at all about the beauty of the temple they all adored. He was more concerned with the condition of their hearts; He wanted them to have a clean heart and a pure spirit within them. He came for those who knew they had need of a Saviour, not those who thought that they were all 'good' because on the outside they looked 'beautiful', just like the outside adornment of a temple.

Jesus was weeping over the city of Jerusalem because He knew that His people were going to reject Him, the Anointed One. Also, those who didn't believe in Him were going to be destroyed by the evil one, the prince of this world, who would come and cause havoc after His death and resurrection, as stated in *Daniel 9:26 and 27:*

> *"After the sixty-nine 'sevens', the Anointed One will be cut off and will have nothing. The people of the ruler who will come will destroy the city and the sanctuary. The end will come like a flood: War will continue until the end, and desolation has been decreed.*

He will confirm a covenant with many for one 'seven' and in the middle of the 'seven', he will put an end to sacrifice and offering. And on a wing of the temple, he will set up an abomination that causes desolation, until the end that is decreed is poured out on him."

Also, Jesus prophesied in *Luke 21:5-7 and 20-24:*

> *"Some of his disciples were remarking about how the temple was adorned with beautiful stones and with gifts dedicated to God. But Jesus said,*
>
> *'As for what you see here, the time will come when not one stone will be left on another; every one of them will be thrown down.'*
>
> *'Teacher,' they asked, 'when will these things happen? And what will be the sign that they are about to take place?'*
>
> *'When you see Jerusalem being surrounded by armies, you will know that the desolation is near. Then let those who are in Judaea flee to the mountains, let those in the city get out; and let those in the country not enter the city.*
>
> *For this is the time of punishment in fulfilment of all that has been written.*
>
> *How dreadful it will be in those days for pregnant women and nursing mothers! There will be great distress in the land and wrath against these people.*
>
> *They will fall by the sword and will be taken as prisoners to all the nations. Jerusalem will be trampled on by the Gentiles until the times of the Gentiles are fulfilled.'"*

In Isaiah 1, the prophet warned the children of Israel what would befall them if they did not take heed to the word of God. What God wanted was for the children of Israel to obey His words and follow His instructions, but they would not listen to and obey Him. So warning was given to them by the prophets from God.

This is what *Isaiah 1:11-20* foretold:

> *"'The multitude of your sacrifices, what are they to me?' says the Lord: 'I have had more than enough burnt offerings of rams and the fat of fatted animals; I have no pleasure in the blood of bulls and lambs, and goats. When ye come to appear before me, who has asked this of you, this trampling of my courts?*
>
> *Stop bringing meaningless offerings! Your incense is detestable to me. New Moons, sabbaths and convocations - I cannot bear your evil assemblies. Your New Moons festivals and your appointed feasts, my soul hates. They have become a burden to me; I am weary of bearing them. When you spread out your hands in prayer, I will hide my eyes from you: even if you offer many prayers, I will not listen. Your hands are full of blood. Wash yourself and make yourselves clean. Take your evil deeds out of my sight! Stop doing wrong.*
>
> *Learn to do it right! Seek justice, encourage the oppressed, defend the cause of the fatherless, plead the case of the widow.'*
>
> *'Come now and let us reason together,' says the Lord. 'Though your sins be like scarlet, they shall be as white as snow; though they are red as crimson, they shall be as wool. If you are willing and obedient, you will eat the best from the land: But if you resist and rebel, you will be devoured by the sword.' For the mouth of the LORD has spoken.*

The Destruction of the Temple

The destruction of the temple and the desolation of Jerusalem came to pass in 70 AD, approximately 38 years after the ascension of Christ.

Deuteronomy 28:47-58 states:

> *"Because you did not serve the Lord your God in joyfulness, and gladly in the time of prosperity, therefore in hunger and thirst, in nakedness and dire poverty, you will serve the enemies the Lord sends against you, he will put a yoke on your neck, until he has destroyed you. The LORD will bring a nation against you from far away, from the end of the earth, like an eagle swooping down, a nation whose language you will not understand, a fierce-looking nation without respect for the old, or pity for the young:*
>
> *They will devour the young of your life-stock, and the crops of your land until you are destroyed. They will leave you no grain, new wine, or oil, nor any calves of your herds or lambs of your flocks until you are ruined.*
>
> *They will lay siege to all the cities throughout your land until the high fortified walls in which you trust fall. They will besiege all the cities throughout the land the Lord your God is giving you.*
>
> *Because of the suffering that your enemy will inflict on you during the siege, you will eat the fruit of your own womb, the flesh of your sons and daughters the Lord your God has given you.*
>
> *Even the most gentle and sensitive man among you will have no compassion on his own brother or the wife he loves or his surviving children, and he will not give to one of them any of the flesh of his children that he is eating. It will be all he had left because of the suffering that your enemy will inflict on you during the siege of all your cities.*
>
> *The most sensitive woman among you – so sensitive and gentle that she would not venture to touch the ground with the sole of her foot – will begrudge the husband she loves and her son or daughter, the afterbirth from her womb and the children she bears. For she*

intends to eat them secretly during the siege and distress that her enemy will inflict in your cities.

If you do not carefully follow all the words of this law, which are written in this book, and do not revere this glorious and awesome name - the Lord your God -.just as it pleased the Lord to make you prosper and increase in number, so it will please him to ruin and destroy you. You will be up-rooted from the land you are entering to possess.

Then the LORD will scatter you among all nations, from one end of the earth to the other. There you will worship other gods – gods of wood and stone, which neither you nor your fathers have known."

These prophetic words spoken in Deuteronomy came to pass and speak of when God's people would be captured and taken from their own land into that of their enemies, because they did not obey God. This is exactly what happened to them, because they disobeyed and sinned.

The siege of Jerusalem in the year 70 AD was the decisive event of the first Jewish-Roman War, in which the Roman army captured the city of Jerusalem and destroyed both the city and its Temple. The Roman army, led by the future Emperor Titus, with Tiberius Julius Alexander as second-in-command, besieged and conquered the city of Jerusalem, which had been controlled by Judean rebel factions since 66 AD, following the Jerusalem riots of 66, when the Judean provisional government was formed in Jerusalem.

According to Josephus, 1.1 million non-combatants died in Jerusalem, mainly because of the violence and famine, but this number exceeds the entire pre-siege population of Jerusalem. Many of the casualties were observant Jews from across the world, such as Babylon and Egypt who travelled to Jerusalem, wanting to celebrate the yearly Passover but instead got trapped in the chaotic siege. He also wrote that 97,000 were enslaved.

The siege of the city began on 14th April 70 AD, three days before the beginning of Passover that year. The siege lasted for about five months; it ended in August 70 AD on Tisha B'Av with the burning and destruction of the second temple. The Romans then entered and sacked the Lower City. The Arch of Titus, celebrating the Roman sack of Jerusalem and the Temple, still stands in Rome. The conquest of the city was completed on approximately 8th September 70 AD.

The siege of Jerusalem was a terrible time in history, because for the Jewish people to survive the wars and famines, they were forced to eat their own children and each other. They were not able to get out of Jerusalem, for they were shut in on every side.

As stated and prophesied in *Matthew 24:21*, *"For then there will be great distress, unequalled from the beginning of the world until now – and never to be equaled again."*

Thus the temple was destroyed a second time. The Romans pulled it down brick by brick so that they would not destroy all the precious stones with which the temple was built. They were removed layer by layer, so they did not leave one stone upon another, as prophesied by Jesus in *Matthew 24:1-2 and Luke 21:5-6.*

1 Kings 9:3-9 states:

> *"The Lord said to him: 'I have heard the prayer and plea you have made before me. I have consecrated this temple, which you have built, by putting my name there forever. Mine eyes and my heart will always be there. As for you, if you walk before me in integrity of heart and uprightness as David your father did, and do all that I command and observe my decrees and laws, I will establish your royal throne over Israel forever, as I promised David your father,*

when I said, 'You shall never fail to have a man on the throne of Israel.'

But if you or your sons turn away from me and do not observe the commands and decrees, I have given you and go off to serve other gods, and worship them,

then I will cut off Israel from the land I have given them and reject this temple I have consecrated for my name. Israel will then be a byword and an object of ridicule among all people:

And though this temple is now imposing, all who pass by will be appalled and will scoff and say, 'Why, has the Lord done such a thing to this land, and to this temple?'

People will answer, 'Because they have forsaken the Lord their God, who brought their fathers out of Egypt, and have embraced other gods, worshipping and serving them – that is why the Lord brought all this disaster on them.'"

THE SECOND QUESTION: "AND WHAT SHALL BE THE SIGN OF THY COMING?"

In *Matthew 24:4-14* we see Jesus reply to His disciples:

"Jesus answered: 'Watch out that no one deceives you. For many will come in my name, claiming, 'I am the Christ,' and will deceive many. You will hear of wars and rumours of wars but see to it that you are not alarmed. Such things must happen, but the end is still to come. Nation will rise against nation, and kingdom against kingdom: there will be famines and earthquakes in various places. All these are the beginning of birth-pains. Then you will be handed over to be persecuted and be put to death and be hated by all nations because of me.

> *At that time many will be turned away from the faith, and will betray and hate each other, and many false prophets will appear and deceive many people.*
>
> *Because of the increase of wickedness, the love of most will grow cold, but he who stands firm to the end, will be saved. And this gospel of the kingdom will be preached in the whole world as a testimony to all nations; and then the end will come.'"*

The disciples asked Jesus, *'What shall be the signs of His coming?' Jesus answered them, saying, 'Take heed that no man deceives you. Many shall come in my name, and shall deceive many.' (Luke 21:8).*

There are many ways that others can try and deceive us - for instance, many may say that they are Christians and deceive many by not following the true words of God. They can camouflage themselves under the banner of Christ and lead many astray from the truth. Many may claim to be Prophets and say they are speaking on God's behalf, but are telling lies as the Lord has not actually spoken to them. They may even perform signs and wonders and cause many to be deceived.

Also, many shall come and will come in the name of Christ and shall deceive many. Because of this, believers of God need to be knowledgeable in the word of God, so that they can spot someone who is a deceiver or counterfeit. A true prophet or follower of God must act in accordance with the word of God.

Wars and Rumours of Wars

From the time of Jesus' ascension until today, there have been many wars and rumours of wars, for example, these many wars :

- In 1914 – 1918 was World War 1, when over 22 million people died.

- In 1915 The Armenian genocide involved the systematic killing and deportation of Armenians by the Turks of the Ottoman Empire. There were over 1 million victims.
- In 1933 the Nazis came to power, and over 6 million Jews were killed in the Holocaust.
- On the 1st September 1939 – 2nd September1945 World War 2 occurred, and over 60 million people died.
- During 1947 – 1991 the Cold War started in 1947 at the end of the 2nd World War and lasted until the dissolution of the Soviet Union on the 26th December 1991.
- On the 25th June 1950 – 27th July 1953 the Korean War happened, where over 5 million people died.
- In 1964 – 1975 we had the Vietnam War, where an estimated over 3 million people died.
- In 1991 there was the Gulf War which began as the Royal Air Force joined allied aircraft in a bombing raid on Iraq and over 600,000 people died.

The word of God declared that nation shall rise against nation, and kingdom against kingdom. This was prophesied long before these wars took place. We have certainly seen this prophetic word come to pass.

The word also tells us that there shall be famines, and earthquakes, in various places, and we have experienced this many times in the world. The Bible predicts that all these are the beginning of birth pains.

Matthew 24 tells us that this will occur.

Earthquakes

Here is a list of some of the earthquakes that the world has seen:

- On Saturday 1st November 1755 there was the Great Lisbon earthquake, which impacted Portugal, on the Feast of all Saints, at around 09.40 local time. In combination with subsequent fires and a tsunami, the earthquake almost destroyed Lisbon and the adjoining area. Its Magnitude was 8.5 – 9, killing over 30,000 people.
  A week after the earthquake, over 90% of the buildings in Lisbon had collapsed and were flooded by the tsunami or burnt by the fires. The destruction included the 70,000-volume royal library, the Royal Ribeira Palace and the whole of Baixa.
- On the 17th October 1989, the Loma Prieta Earthquake struck the San Francisco Bay area, in California, U.S.A. This caused 63 deaths, nearly 3,800 injuries, and an estimated $6 billion in property damage.
- Hurricane Hugo inflicted widespread damage across the Northeastern Caribbean and Southeastern United States in September 1989. Across its tract, Hugo affected approximately 2 million people. Its direct effect killed 67 people and inflicted $11 billion in damages.

There have been many more earthquakes, in diverse places all over the world.

Famines

Here is a partial list of some famines that have occurred in the world:

- During 1315 – 1317 the Great Famine occurred in Europe when potato crops failed.

- From 1601 – 1603 Russia's worst famine killed approximately two million people.
- From 1630 – 1632 in Deccan Plateau, India there was a famine that was a result of three consecutive staple crop failures.
- From 1740 – 1741 there was the Irish Famine, which resulted in a greater loss than the famine of 1845-1852.
- From 1769 – 1773 The Great Bengal Famine affected the lower Gangetic plain of India from Bihar to the western Bengal region.
- In 1845 – 1852 the Great Famine occurred in Ireland when Ireland's potato crop failed for a number of successive years.
- In 1891 – 1892 The Great Famine of Russia, due to the dry autumn delayed the seeding of the fields.
- In 1917 – 1919 during the Great Famine of Persia, as many as eight to ten million Persian perished because of starvation and disease.
- In 1959 – 1961 during the Great China Famine, over 15-55 million people died.

These are but a few famines from all over the world that caused many deaths over the years.

<u>Division of Nations, Families, and Believers</u>

> *"Then you will be handed over to be persecuted and put to death: and you will be hated by all nations because of me. At that time many will turn away from the faith and will betray and hate each other." (Matthew 24:9-10).*

Through the ages since the ascension of Jesus, many people have been killed and been persecuted because of the name of Jesus, and because of their faith in Jesus. Even in our present society, many around the world are being killed, put in prison, and tortured for their belief in the name of Jesus.

The reason for this is given in *John 16:3-4,* which says:

> *"They will do such things because they have not known the Father or Me.*
>
> *I have told you this, so that when the time comes you will remember that I warned you. I did not tell you this at first because I was with you."*

As the time of the coming of Jesus' return is approaching, many people who are Christians, because of the fear of being persecuted will be offended and will betray one another and hate one another. Also, many false prophets will arise, and shall deceive many.

We can see even in our society today and via social media, that many people say that they are prophets, and are confusing many with their words. They are claiming, for example, that God told them in their dreams about His coming and what one should do or not do, and many are just believing them without question or discernment.

The word of God confirms this with these words, *"Therefore, because wickedness shall abound or increase, the love of many shall grow cold. But he that endure unto the end, the same shall be saved. And this gospel of the kingdom shall be preached in all the world for a testimony unto all nations; and then shall the end come." (Matthew 24:11-14).*

The gospel of the kingdom is now being preached all over the world, more than at any other time in history. Because of the internet, people can access the gospel on social media, for instance via online newspapers, books, Facebook, YouTube, Instagram, the Internet and from the convenience of their phones. Even children now have access to their own phones. The gospel can be accessed from anywhere or wherever one may be. Satellites are now being used to spread the gospel all over the world. It is clear to see that what Jesus told his disciples would happen before the end comes, is being fulfilled.

Matthew 24:22-28 also stated that:

> *"If those days had not been cut short, no-one would have survived, but for the sake of the elect those days will be shortened. At that time if anyone says to you, 'Look, here is the Christ' or, 'There he is!' do not believe it.*
>
> *For false Christs, and false prophets will appear and perform great signs and miracles to deceive even the elect – if that was possible. See, I have told you ahead of time.*
>
> *So, if anyone tells you, 'There he is, or say unto you, He is out in the desert,' do not go out; or, 'Here he is, in the inner rooms,' do not believe it.*
>
> *For as lightning that comes from the east is visible even in the west, so will be the coming of the Son of Man. Wherever there is a carcass there the vultures will gather."*

First, we were told by Jesus that for His elect's sake, the time will be shortened. We can all agree today that the world is experiencing the fulfilment of this, for even children are saying how fast the time is going. We give thanks to God for doing this on our behalf, that many of us can have access to the kingdom of God during this time of great persecution, which has come and will continue to come upon us; Jesus though, has made a way of escape.

As Jesus stated, unless those days are shortened, then many would not be saved. He also told us that if any man shall tell us that *'here is the Christ, or there' we are not to believe it, because false Christs and false prophets will arise and will show great signs and wonders; and if it were possible, they would deceive the very elect.* Jesus is warning us to be on our guard. For as the lightning comes out of the east, and shines even to the west, so shall the coming of the Son of man be. All shall be aware of His coming at the same time.

THE THIRD QUESTION: "WHAT SHALL BE THE SIGN OF THE END OF THE AGE?"

In *Matthew 24:29-36*, Jesus continued His reply to the disciples:

> *"Immediately after the distress of those days, 'the sun will be darkened, and the moon will not give its light, the stars will fall from the sky, and the heavenly bodies will be shaken.'*
>
> *At that time the sign of the Son of Man will appear in the sky, and all nations of the earth will mourn. They will see the Son of Man coming on the clouds of the sky, with power and great glory. And he will send his angels with a loud trumpet call, and they shall gather his elect from the four winds, from one end of the heaven to the other.*
>
> *Now learn this lesson from the fig tree: As soon as its twigs get tender and leaves come out, you know that summer is near: Even so when you see all these things, you know it is near, right at the door. I tell you the truth, this generation will certainly not pass away until all these things have happened. Heaven and earth will pass away, but my words will never pass away.*
>
> *No-one knows about that day or hour, not even the angels in heaven, nor the Son, but only the Father."*

THE SEQUENCE OF EVENTS LEADING UP TO JESUS' RETURN

At Christ's coming, the Bible tells us that the whole world will be covered in darkness. It will bring us back to the time of creation, when darkness was upon the face of the deep.

> *"The sun will be darkened. It will not give her light on the earth anymore, nor will the moon, and the stars fall from heaven onto the earth: for the powers of heaven shall be shaken." (see Matthew 24:29).*

It will be a time of great mourning, as the people living on earth at this time will be in great fear of what they see coming upon the earth. They will see the Son of Man coming in the clouds of heaven with power and great glory, as stated in *Matthew 24:30.*

God will send his angels with the sound of a trumpet and they shall gather together his elect from the four winds, from one end of heaven to the other. This means from the north, the south, the east, and the west, the whole world. *(see Matthew 24:31).*

Believers will be experiencing a time of jubilee when Jesus comes to receive them to Himself. They will be taken out of the persecution they have been enduring and be liberated from all their trials. Jesus will come and fight for His children and deliver them from the grip of satan, and take them home to heaven, to live with Him forever.

In *Matthew 24:32-33* Jesus drew the disciples' attention to learn the parable of the fig tree. He said to them, *'Now learn the lesson from the fig tree. As soon as its twigs get tender and its leaves come out, you know that summer is near.*

Even so, when you see all these things, you know that it is near, right at the door.'

This is telling us we will know He is coming soon when we see coming to pass all that Jesus said in His words, for example:

- The gospel being preached in all the world for a testimony against all nations.
- People coming in the disguise of Christ and even performing many miracles.
- The shortening of the times.
- Persecution of the Body of Christ on a large scale.
- The heavenly bodies being shaken.

Then we will know for sure that His coming is close - even at the door. Jesus said that with these occurrences, if it were possible, even the very elect would be deceived.

"He continued, *'This generation shall not pass away until all has happened. Heaven and earth will pass away, but my words will never pass away,'" (Matthew 24:33-34).*

The disciples then and all those after them, right up to His coming, are given warning, that they are to watch, for no man knows the day nor the hour when Jesus will return, not even the angels of heaven, but the Father only. *(Matthew 24:36).*

This does not mean that Jesus does not know, for the Father is God, and so is Jesus. Jesus said that He and His Father are one. *(John 10:30).*

Parables Concerning Jesus' Coming

Below are some more parables that Jesus gave concerning His coming:

Matthew 24:37-44 states:

> *"As it was in the days of Noah, so will it be at the coming of the Son of Man. For in the days before the flood, people were eating and drinking, marrying, and giving in marriage, up to the day Noah entered the ark and they knew nothing about what would happen until the flood came and took them all away. That is how it will be at the coming of the Son of Man. Two men will be in the field; one will be taken, and the other left. Two women will be grinding with a hand mill; one will be taken and the other left. Therefore, keep watch, because you do not know on what day your Lord will come.*
>
> *But understand this: If the owner of the house had known at what time of the night the thief was coming, he would have kept watch and would not have let his house be broken into. So, you also must be ready, because the Son of Man will come at an hour when you do not expect him."*

When the angels start to do the reaping, they shall collect the unbelievers first and put them in a separate place, from the believers.

In *Matthew 13:24-30* Jesus told them another parable,

> *"The kingdom of heaven is like a man who sowed good seed in his field. But while everyone was sleeping, his enemy came and sowed weeds among the wheat, and went his way. When the wheat sprouted and formed ears, then the weeds also appeared.*
>
> *The owner's servants came to him and said, 'Sir, did you sow good seed in your field? Where did the weeds come from?'*
>
> *'An enemy did this,' he replied.*
>
> *The servants asked him, 'Do you want us to go and pull them up?'*

'No,' he answered, 'because while you are pulling the weeds, you may root up the wheat with them. Let both grow together until the harvest: At that time, I will tell the harvesters: First collect the weeds and tie them in bundles to be burned; then gather the wheat and bring them into my barn.'"

Matthew 13:36-42, states:

"Then Jesus left the crowd and went into the house. His disciples came unto him and said, 'Explain to us the parable of the weeds in the field.'

He answered, 'The one who sowed the good seed is the Son of Man. The field is the world, and the good seeds are the sons of the kingdom. The weeds are the sons of the evil one, and the enemy who sows them is the devil. The harvest is the end of the age, and the harvesters are the angels. As the weeds are pulled up and burned in the fire, so will it be at the end of this age. The Son of man will send out his angels, and they will weed out of his kingdom everything that causes sin, and all who do evil. They will throw them into the fiery furnace, where there will be weeping and gnashing of teeth.'"

Here it is clear that the weeds are gathered first and taken out of the world to be destroyed, as mentioned in *Matthew 24:37-42* above and in *Luke 17:26-27* below:

"Just as it was in the days of Noah, so also will be in the days of the Son of Man. People were eating, drinking, marrying, and were given in marriage up to the day Noah entered the ark. Then the flood came and destroyed them all."

Luke 17: 34 also states:

> *"I tell you, on that night two people will be in one bed; one will be taken, and the other left."*

This signifies that two people in a bed refer to those in the graves. The unbelieving one shall be taken to be destroyed, and the believing one will be left to be with Jesus forever.

Then two shall be in the field, which represent both the good and the evil ones in the world. The ones that did not accept the salvation of Jesus Christ and those that did. The angels will gather the evil ones for burning, while the good ones who obeyed the instruction of God's word and accepted His salvation will be left. (*see Matthew 24:40.)*

Two women shall be grinding at the mill. These groups represent the two churches: the unfaithful church and the faithful church. The unfaithful church shall be taken away to be destroyed and the faithful church will remain. The grinding at the mill refers to two women making bread. The bread here represents Jesus, the Bread of Life. The church is the body of Christ that should be feeding the world with the life giving bread, which is the true words of God. *(see Matthew 24:41 & Luke 17:35).*

The Bible says that two women will be grinding grain together; one will be taken, and the other left.

Matthew 25: 1-10 states,

> *"At that time the kingdom of heaven will be like ten virgins, who took their lamps and went out to meet the bridegroom. Five of them were foolish, and five were wise. The foolish ones took their lamps but did not take any oil with them.,*

> *The wise, however, took oil in jars along with their lamps. The bridegroom was a long time in coming, and they all became drowsy and fell asleep.*
>
> *At midnight the cry rang out: 'Here's the bridegroom! Come out to meet him!'*
>
> *Then all the virgins woke up and trimmed their lamps.*
>
> *The foolish ones said to the wise, 'Give us some of your oil; our lamps are going out.'*
>
> *'No,' they replied, 'there may not be enough for both us and you. Instead, go to those who sell oil and buy some for yourselves.'*
>
> *But while they were on their way to buy the oil, the bridegroom arrived. The virgins who were ready went in with him to the wedding banquet. And the door was shut."*

Five were foolish, and five were wise; the wise ones carried extra oil with them, which represents the Holy Spirit, and the foolish ones carried no oil with them, signifying that they did not have the Holy Spirit in them. The foolish ones were left behind, while the wise ones went with the bridegroom to the wedding banquet.

Jesus also likened the kingdom of heaven to a net in *Matthew 13:47-50:*

> *"Once again, the kingdom of heaven is like a net that was let down into the lake to catch all kinds of fish. When it was full, the fishermen pulled it up on the shore. Then they sat down and collected the good fish in baskets but threw the bad away. This is how it will be at the end of the age. The angels will come and separate the wicked from the righteous and throw them into the fiery furnace, where there will be weeping and gnashing of teeth."*

Matthew 24:48-51 states:

> *"But suppose that servant is wicked and says to himself, 'My master is staying away a long time, and he then begins to beat his fellow servants and to eat and drink with the drunkards. The master of that servant will come on a day when he does not expect him, and at an hour he is not aware of. He will cut him in pieces and assign him a place with the hypocrites, where there will be weeping and gnashing of teeth."*

The evil ones will be stirring up havoc with the children of God. Persecution will be rife against God's children, that they will feel as if they are in bondage. This will be taking place all around the world, including the beloved city Jerusalem.

There will not be anywhere on earth that will be left out from this time of persecution. Many people are being killed and will be killed, and Satan will be thinking he is winning the battle, but Jesus will rescue all his followers with the sword of his mouth, which is the word of God.

Revelation 20:8-10 says to us:

> *"Satan will go out to deceive the nations in the four corners of the earth - Gog and Magog - to gather them for battle. In number they are like the sand on the seashore. They marched across the breath of the earth and surrounded the camp of God's people, the city he loves. But fire came down from heaven and devoured them. And the devil, who deceived them, was thrown into the lake of burning sulphur, where the beast and false prophet had been thrown. They will be tormented day and night for ever and ever."*

Jesus will now return to liberate His Saints. He will overthrow the works and plans of Satan, and he will be punished. Satan will not be able to deceive the world any longer, for he will be seen for who he really is. Sadly, all who were deceived by him will mourn, and wail as they see it's too late, that because of him they have lost out on eternal life.

Revelation 19:17-21, tells us:

> *"And I saw an angel standing in the sun, and he cried with a loud voice, saying to all the fowls that fly, in the midst of heaven, 'Come and gather yourselves together unto the supper of the great God.'*
>
> *That they may eat the flesh of kings, and the flesh of captains, and the flesh of mighty men, and the flesh of horses, and them that sit on them, and the flesh of all men, both free and bond, both small and great.*
>
> *And I saw the beast, and the kings of the earth, and their armies, gathered to make war against him that sat on the horse, and against his army.*
>
> *And the beast was taken, and with him the false prophet that wrought miracles before him, with which he deceived them that had received the mark of the beast, and them that worshipped his image. These both were cast alive into a lake of fire burning with brimstone.*
>
> *And the remnant was slain with the sword of him that sat upon the horse, which sword proceeded out of his mouth: and all the fowls were filled with their flesh."*

This is what awaits those who have not accepted the gift of salvation that is given to everyone freely. Jesus paid the price for our sin, died on the cross of Calvary so that all could have eternal life. Those who do the bidding of the evil one are those who carried the mark of the beast in their hearts and carried out his evil deeds.

Matthew 24:44-47 tells us more and says:

> *"Therefore, be also ready: for in such an hour as you think not the son of man cometh. Who then is a faithful and wise servant, whom his lord hath made ruler over his household, to give them meat in due season? Blessed is that servant, whom his lord when he comes shall find so doing. Verily I say unto you, that he shall make him ruler over all his goods."*

When Jesus returns, He will be coming in the fullness of His glory. He will be returning in the clouds of heaven, with His angels and ten thousand of his saints, to perform judgement on the earth.

As stated in *Revelation 1:10, 12-16,* John the Revealer informs us what Jesus the Son of man looks like in heaven:

> *"I was in the Spirit on the Lord's day and heard behind me a great voice, as if of a trumpet. And I turned to see the voice that spoke with me. And being turned, I saw seven golden candlesticks. And in the midst of the seven candlesticks one like unto the son of man. Clothed with a garment down to the foot and grit about the waist with a golden girdle. His head and his hairs were white like wool, as white as snow, and his eyes were as a flame of fire: And his feet like unto fine brass, as if they burned in a furnace; and his voice as the sound of many waters.*
>
> *And he had in his right hand seven stars: and out of his mouth went a sharp two-edged sword: and his countenance was as the sun shineth in his strength."*

From the appearance of Jesus, when He returns, the heaven and earth in its present form shall be removed out of its place. The angels will do the reaping and separate the bad from the good, the unbelievers from the believers, and the weeds from the wheat. The weeds will face the white throne of judgement, and the second death, and the wheat be united with Christ in the new Jerusalem in heaven.

Revelation 19:11-16 tells us what will happen:

> *"I saw heaven standing open and there before me was a white horse, whose rider is called Faithful and True. With justice he judges and makes war. His eyes are like blazing fire, and on his head are many crowns. He has a name written on him that no-one knows but he himself. He is dressed in a robe dipped in blood, and his name is the Word of God. The armies of heaven were following him, riding on white horses and dressed in fine linen, white and clean.*
>
> *Out of his mouth comes a sharp sword with which to strike down the nations. He will rule them with a rod of iron sceptre. He treads the winepress of the fury of the wrath of God Almighty. On his robe and on his thigh, he has this name written: KING OF KINGS AND LORD OF LORDS."*

On Jesus' return, the brightness of his countenance shall slay the wicked, the unbelieving ones. There will not be any unbelievers left alive for they will be dead and awaiting the white throne judgement and the second death. The Bible says that the fowls of heaven shall eat up their flesh.

Revelation 19:17-21 describes what will happen here:

> *"And I saw an angel standing in the sun, who cried in a loud voice, to all the birds flying in mid-air, of heaven, 'Come, gather-together for the great supper of God, so that you may eat the flesh of kings, generals, and mighty men, of horses and their riders, and the flesh of all people, free and slave, small and great.'*

Then I saw the beast and the kings of the earth, and their armies gathered together to make war against the rider on the horse, and his army. But the beast was captured, and with him the false prophet who performed the miraculous signs on his behalf. With these signs he deluded those who received the mark of the beast and worshipped his image. The two of them were thrown alive into the fiery lake of burning sulphur.

The rest of them were killed with the sword that came out of the mouth of the rider on the horse, and all the birds gorged themselves on their flesh."

When the trumpet of God shall sound, the angels would have already sealed all believers who are alive. The believing ones, who had died, will be raised first, they with the living ones will be caught up to meet Jesus in the air.

They shall both change from mortals to immortality in a twinkling of an eye, or in a moment. The living will not prevent those who are asleep or who have died, as stated in *1 Thessalonian 4:14-17:*

"We believe that Jesus died and rose again and so we believe that God will bring with Jesus those who have fallen asleep in him. According to the Lord's own word, He will tell you that we who are still alive, who are left till the coming of the Lord, will certainly not precede those who have fallen asleep.

For the Lord himself will come down from heaven, with a loud command, with the voice of the archangel and with the trumpet call of God, and the dead in Christ will rise first. After that, we who are still alive and are left will be caught up together with them in the clouds to meet the Lord in the air. And so, we will be with the Lord forever."

Revelation 20:11-15 then says:

> *"Then I saw a great white throne and him who was seated on it. Earth and sky fled from his presence, and there was no place for them. And I saw the dead, great and small, standing before the throne of God, and books were opened. Another book was opened, which is the book of life. The dead were judged according to what they had done, as recorded in the books.*
>
> *The sea gave up the dead that were in it, and death and Hades gave up the dead that were in them, and each person was judged according to what he had done.*
>
> *Then death and Hades were thrown into the lake of fire. This lake of fire is the second death. If anyone's name was not found written in the book of life, he was thrown into the lake of fire."*

Revelation 21:8 states:

> *"But the cowardly, the unbelieving, the vile, the murderers, the sexually immoral, those who practise magic arts, the idolaters, and all liars - their place will be in the fiery lake of burning sulphur. This is the second death."*

This is the last state of all unbelievers, for they will meet the full punishment of the judgement of God for not accepting His Son and the free gifts of salvation, offered to one and all.

Matthew 13:43 tells us what happens to the righteous here:

> *"Then the righteous will shine like the sun in the kingdom of their Father. He who has ears, let him hear."*
>
> *And Revelation 21:1-7 also tells us what awaits us as His believers:*

> *"Then I saw a new heaven and a new earth, for the first heaven and the first earth had passed away, and there was no longer any sea. I saw the Holy City, the new Jerusalem, coming down out of heaven from God, prepared as a bride beautifully dressed for her husband.*
>
> *And I heard a loud voice from the throne saying, 'Now, the dwelling of God is with men, and he will live with them, and be their God. He will wipe every tear from their eyes. There will be no more death, or mourning or crying, or pain, for the old order of things has passed away.'*
>
> *He who was seated on the throne said, 'I am making everything new.' Then he said, 'Write it down, for these words are trustworthy and true.'*
>
> *He said to me: 'It is done. I am the Alpha and Omega, the Beginning, and the End. To him who is thirsty I will give to drink without cost from the spring of the living water of life.'*
>
> *He who overcomes will inherit all this, and I will be his God, and he will be my son."*

The saints will be called the sons of God; we shall become like the angels in heaven.

See Matthew 22:23-32 which states:

> *"That same day the Sadducees, who say there is no resurrection, came to him with a question. 'Teacher,' they said, 'Moses told us that if a man dies without having children, his brother must marry his widow, and have children for him.*
>
> *Now there were seven brothers among us, the first one married and died, and since he had no children, he left his wife to his brother. The same thing happens to the second and third brother, right down*

to the seventh. Finally, the woman died. Now then at the resurrection, whose wife will she be of the seven since all of them were married to her?'

Jesus replies, 'You are in error because you do not know the scriptures or the power of God. At the resurrection people will neither marry, nor be given in marriage: they will be like angels in heaven. But about the resurrection of the dead - have you not read what God said to you, 'I am the God of Abraham, the God of Isaac, and the God of Jacob'? He is not the God of the dead but the living.'"

From Jesus' response to the Sadducees, the saints can now see what they will be, that they will become the bride of Christ. They shall be like angels. Let's see what an angel in heaven looked like.

Daniel 10:5 – 6 says:

"I lifted my eyes and looked and there before me was a man dressed in linen, with a belt of the finest gold round his waist. His body was like chrysolite, his face like lightning, his eyes like flaming torches, his arms and legs like the gleam of burnished bronze, and his voice like the sound of a multitude."

This is a description of an angel, seen by Daniel during one of his visions. He is informing us what we shall be like when Jesus returns to take His redeemed one's home to heaven to live with Him.

Praise God, we have this to look forward to!

APPENDIX I

QUESTIONS AND ANSWERS FOR FURTHER STUDY

Bible Study Questions based on Daniel's 70 weeks vision in Daniel 9:1-27

1. Who was reigning in Babylon when Daniel had his vision about the 70 "Sevens" or (70 weeks) prophecy?
2. What was revealed to Daniel about what was happening to his people when he was reading the Scriptures in the book of Jeremiah the prophets?
3. Why was Daniel distressed when he came across this Scripture?
4. What did Daniel do to try and remedy the situation?
5. Did God answer Daniel?
6. What was the answer God gave to Daniel to give him comfort?
7. How many years are the 70 weeks (seventy 'sevens') vision representing?
8. Where in the Bible does it state a day represents a year in prophecy?

9. What time within this seventy 'sevens' will the Anointed One be cut off?

10. What will happen to Jerusalem after the Anointed One is put to death?

11. Who are Daniel's people?

12. Daniel 9:27 says,
He will confirm a covenant with many for one 'seven.' In the middle of 'seven' he will put an end to sacrifice and offering. And at the temple he will set up an abomination that causes desolation, until the end that is decreed is poured out on him.
Who is this scripture talking about?

13. Was the above prophecy fulfilled?

14. When was it fulfilled?

15. What happened after the last part of the final 'seven.' Was it fulfilled?

Answers to the bible questions based on Daniel 9:1-27

1. Darius's son of Ahasuerus a Mede by Descent.
2. The desolation of Jerusalem would last 70 years.
3. The time of the 70 years desolation i.e. captivity of Babylon was coming to an end, but his people were still walking in the part that carries the curse instead of the blessing.
4. He pours out his soul to God in prayer and fasting in sackcloth and ashes, confessing his sins and the sins of his people, asking God for mercy and forgiveness of his and his people's sins, and for God to turn away His wrath and anger from Jerusalem.
5. Yes.
6. Daniel 9:25-26
   Seventy 'sevens' (490 years) are decreed for your people and your holy city to finish transgression, to put an end to sin, to atone for wickedness, to bring in everlasting righteousness, to seal up the vision and prophecy and to anoint the Most Holy Place. Know and understand this: From the time the word goes out to restore and rebuild Jerusalem until the Anointed One, the ruler, comes, there will be seven 'seven,' (49 years) and sixty-two 'sevens.' (434 years) It will be rebuilt with a trench, but in times of trouble.
7. 490 years.
8. Numbers 14:34 and Ezekiel 4:6.
9. After the sixty-two 'sevens,' in the middle of the last 7 years the Anointed One will be put to death and will have nothing. Jesus was put to death 3 and a ½ years after His anointing.

10. The people of the ruler who will come will destroy the city and the sanctuary. The end will come like a flood: War will continue until the end, and desolation has been decreed. In 70 AD the Romans would fulfill this prophecy and destroy the temple and Jerusalem.

11. Judah and Benjamin.

12. Jesus at His crucifixion.

13. Yes

14. AD 70 when the Romans invaded Jerusalem and destroyed the second Temple.

15. The gospel was taken to the Samaritans and the Gentiles (all have access to the free gifts of God's salvation plan.) The final year 'one of seven', (Acts 7 & Acts 8:4-5) explained the persecution and death of Stephen. The 70 weeks '70' 'seven' vision was now completed. The 490 years given to Daniel's people had expired.

Bible Study Questions based on Nebuchadnezzar's, Daniel's and John the Revealer's dreams and visions

Nebuchadnezzar's Dream

1. Why did Nebuchadnezzar want all his magicians, enchanters, sorcerers and astrologers and the wise men of Babylon killed?
2. Was Nebuchadnezzar fair in wanting his wise men killed?
3. Why was he not fair in commanding this act?
4. What did Daniel and his three companions do to escape the king's command to kill them along with his wise men?
5. What was the outcome of Daniel and his three companions when they consulted their God for mercy?
6. What is the name of Daniel's three companions?
7. How did Daniel respond to God for revealing the mystery of Nebuchadnezzar's dream to him?
8. Why did Daniel ask Arioch not to execute the wise men of Babylon?
9. How was the dream revealed to Daniel?
10. What was Daniel's Babylonian name?
11. What was the new name given to Hananiah, Mishael and Azariah?
12. Why was Nebuchadnezzar given the dream he could not remember by God?
13. What did Nebuchadnezzar dream about?

14. What did he see in his dream?
15. What was the interpretation of his dream?
16. What did Nebuchadnezzar give to Daniel and his three companions for the revelation and interpretation of his dream?

Answers to bible questions on Nebuchadnezzar's Dream

1. He wanted his wise men killed because they couldn't reveal to him what his dream was or its meaning.
2. No.
3. No human can tell what another human's dreams are, unless it was revealed by God.
4. They asked Arioch the commander to request time from the king for them to pray and ask their God to reveal the dream and its interpretation to them.
5. God revealed the mystery of the dream and meaning to Daniel.
6. Hananiah, Mishael and Azariah.
7. Daniel praised the God of heaven and said: "Praise be to the name of God for ever and ever; Wisdom and power are His. He changes time and seasons; He deposes kings and raises others. He gives wisdom to the wise and knowledge to the discerning. He reveals deep and hidden things; He knows what lies in darkness, and light dwells with Him. I thank and praise You, God of my ancestors. You have given me wisdom and power; You have made known to me that which we have asked You. You have made known to us the dream of the king." (Daniel 2:19b-23).
8. God has revealed the dream and meaning to him.
9. During the night it was revealed to Daniel in a vision.
10. Belteshazzar.
11. To Hananiah, Shadrach; to Mishael, Meshach; and to Azariah, Abednego.

12. The king was in bed and his thoughts wandered to what would happen in the days to come. So, God revealed this mystery to him in a dream.

13. What was going to happen in the world during his reign, and after, right up to the coming of Christ.

14. *Your majesty looked, and there before you stood a large statue – an enormous, dazzling statue, awesome in appearance. The head of the statue was made of pure gold, its chest and arms of silver, its belly and thighs of bronze, its legs of iron, its feet partly of iron, and partly of baked clay. While you were watching, a rock was cut out, but not by human hands. It struck the statue on its feet of iron and clay and smashed them. Then the iron, the clay, the bronze, the silver and the gold were all broken to pieces and became like chaff on a threshing floor in the summer. The wind swept them away without leaving a trace. But the rock that struck the statue became a huge mountain and filled the whole earth. (Daniel 2:31-35).*

15. *Your majesty, you are the king of kings. The God of heaven has given you dominion and power and might and glory; In your hands He has placed all mankind and beasts of the field and the birds of the sky. Wherever they live, He made you ruler over them all. You are that head of gold.*
    "After you another kingdom will rise inferior to yours. Next a third kingdom, one of bronze, will rule over the whole earth. Finally, a fourth kingdom, strong as iron – for iron breaks things to pieces, so it will crush and break all the others. Just as you saw that the feet and toes were partly of baked clay and partly of iron, so this will be a divided kingdom; Yet it will have some of the strength of iron in it, even as you saw iron mixed with clay. So, the kingdom will be partly strong and partly brittle. Just as you saw, the iron mixed with baked clay, the people will be a mixture and will not

remain united any more than iron mixes with clay. In the time of those kings, the God of heaven will set up his kingdom that will never be destroyed, nor will it be left to another people. It will crush all those kingdoms and bring them to an end, but it will itself endure forever. This is the meaning of the vision of the rock cut out of a mountain, but not with human hands – A rock that broke the iron, the bronze, the clay, the silver and the gold to pieces. The great God has shown the king what will take place in the future. The dream is true, and its interpretation is trustworthy." (Daniel 2:37-45).

16. *King Nebuchadnezzar prostrated before Daniel and paid him honor and ordered that an offering and incense be presented to him. The king said to Daniel, "Surely your God is the God of gods and the Lord of kings and a revealer of mysteries, for you were able to reveal this mystery."*
    The king placed Daniel in a high position and lavished many gifts on him. He made him ruler over the entire province of Babylon and placed him in charge of all its wise men. Moreover, at Daniel's request the king appointed Shadrach, Meshach and Abednego as administrators over the province of Babylon, while Daniel himself remained at the royal court. (Daniel 2:46-49.)

Bible Questions on Daniel and John the Revealer's dreams and visions

Daniel 7-8 and Revelation

1. In the first year of Belshazzar, king of Babylon Daniel had a dream, and visions. What did Daniel first see in this vision?
2. In Daniel's vision he saw four beasts come out of the sea. Can you name those four beasts?
3. What did the first beast look like?
4. What happened to the eagle's wing that was on the lion?
5. What happened to the lion after its wing was torn off?
6. Describe the second beast?
7. What was the second beast told to do?
8. What did the three ribs in its mouth represent?
9. Who was the first nation the beast that looked like a bear captured?
10. How was the second beast able to capture the first beast?
11. What are the names of the kings who were reigning when Babylon was captured?
12. What happened to King Belshazzar?
13. Describe the third beast?
14. Which nation is the third beast?
15. What do the four wings and four heads on the third beast represent?
16. These beasts that the bible mentions, are symbolic of what?
17. The beasts that come up out of the sea, what does it represent?

18. The fourth beast who was terrifying and frightening and very powerful, had iron teeth and crushed and devoured its victims and trampled underfoot whatever was left represented which nation?
19. How many horns did the fourth beast have?
20. What do the ten horns represent?
21. Among the 10 horns another little horn came up among them, who does the little horn represent that three of the first horns were rooted up before it?
22. What was the name of the dragon who gave his power to the beast?
23. Who was the beast that got its power from the dragon?
24. In Daniel's vision, who will eventually possess the kingdom?
25. In Daniel's vision whose throne was set in place?
26. What did the Ancient of Days look like?
27. What was happening around the Ancient of Days throne?
28. What do you think was taking place around the throne?
29. Who does the boastful horn represent?
30. How long was Papal Rome in power according to the bible?
31. How long did Pagan Rome rule?
32. In which year Papal Rome began?
33. How long did Papal Rome rule?
34. How did Papal Rome get its deadly wound that came to an end?
35. Which nation separated Church and State from under Papal Rome control?
36. When was Sunday worship introduced?

37. By whom was Sunday worship introduced?

38. Daniel 7:11

    Then I continued to watch because of the boastful words the horn was speaking. I kept looking until the beast was slain and its body destroyed and thrown into the blazing fire.

    a. Which beast is the above scripture talking about?

    b. When did this fulfilment take place?

    c. Who was the horn speaking boastfully?

39. Who did Daniel in his vision see coming in the cloud of heaven?

40. Who is it that was one like the Son of Man?

41. When will the saints possess the kingdom?

42. Which kingdom will the saints possess?

43. Will Jesus ever come and live on this earth again, yes, or no?

44. If the answer to question 43 is No, why do you think this?

45. For how long will the holy people be given into the hands of this beast?

46. Can you calculate this time span, time, times and half a time?

47. Where in the bible can you find the above confirmation on question 45?

48. Under whose rule will Christ Jesus return?

49. Who does the fourth kingdom represent?

50. Who are the 10 horns and the seven heads?

Answers to bible questions on Daniel and John the Revealer's dreams & visions.

1. He saw before him the four wings of heaven churning up the great sea. And four great beasts, each different from the others, came out of the sea.

2.
    a. First looked like a lion
    b. Second looked like a bear.
    c. Third looked like a leopard.
    d. Fourth was terrifying, frightening and very powerful.

3. The first beast looked like a lion, and it had the wings of an eagle.

4. The wing of the lion was torn off.

5. The lion was lifted from the ground so that it stood on two feet like a human being, and the mind of a human was given to it.

6. The second beast looks like a bear. It raised up on one of its sides, and it had three ribs in its mouth between its teeth.

7. The second beast was told 'To get up and eat its fill of flesh.'

8. The three ribs in his mouth are Egypt which is Southward, Lydia which is Westward, and Babylon which is Northward. (Daniel 8:4)

9. The beast who looks like a bear captured Babylon.

10. The first beast that was captured (Babylon) by the second beast (Mede and Percia) the Euphrates River dried up because of drought, and the gate of the City being left open while the king and his officials were having a party. (Daniel 5:1, 30-31)

11. King Belshazzar and his father King Nabonidus ruled when their kingdom was captured.

12. King Belshazzar was killed the same night Babylon was overthrown by the Medes and Persians. (Daniel 5:30-31}

13. The third beast looked like a leopard. On its back it had four wings like those of a bird. This beast had four heads, and it was given authority to rule.

14. Greece.

15. The nation of Greece was run by Alexander the Great. The four wings and four heads represented the four generals who ruled after his death.

16. Nations, Kingdoms, Rulers and those in Authority. (Daniel 8:20-22}

17. The sea represents water. Revelation 17-15: The waters you saw, where the prostitute sits, are peoples, multitudes, nations and languages.

18. The fourth beast is Rome.

19. The fourth beast had Ten horns.

20. The 10 horns represent ten nations which are:
    - Alemanni – Germany
    - Franks – French
    - Burgundians – Switzerland
    - Suevi – Portugal
    - Vandals - The Vandals were a Germanic Tribe that originated in Scandinavia and migrated across Europe

- Visigoths – Spain
- Anglo-Saxons – England
- Ostrogoths - The Ostrogoths were a Germanic people who established the Ostrogothic Kingdom of Italy, which controlled Italy and neighboring area from 493 AD to 553 AD
- Lombard – Italy
- Heruli - The Heruli were an East Germanic people originally from Scandinavia

21. Papal Rome. (The Vatican) (Daniel 7:8, 20, 24-25).
22. The dragon is Pagan Rome. (civil and political power).
23. Papal Rome got its power from Pagan Rome. In 538 ADS, when Emperor Justinian gave his power to Pope Vigilius.
24. The Saints of God shall possess the kingdom. (Daniel 8:22 & 27)
25. The Ancient of Days throne was set in place.
26. The Ancient of Days clothing was white as snow; the hair of His head was white like wool.
27. The Ancient of Days throne was flaming with fire, and its wheels were all ablaze. A river of fire was flowing before Him. Thousands upon thousands attended Him; Ten thousand times ten thousand stood before Him. The court was seated, and the books were opened. (Daniel 7:10).
28. God's end time judgement.
29. The boastful horn represents Papal Rome. (Daniel 7:20, 25)

30. Papal Rome had unbroken power, (Time, times and divided of time (3 1/2 years), (Daniel 7:25, Revelation 12:14}, 42 months (Revelation 13:5), and 1260 days (Revelation 12:6), (but in prophetic terms a year for a day, so 1,260 years), see (Numbers 14:34 and Ezekiel 4:5-6).

31. Over 1000 years, (from 753 BC to 476 AD) (The Roman Empire was from 27 BC to 476 AD). Pagan Rome ended in 538 AD in the West. It was taken over by Papal Rome in 538 AD in the west and in 1453 AD it was taken over by the Byzantine Empire from Constantinople in the East.

32. Papal Rome began in 538 AD.

33. Papal Rome ruled for 1260 years from 538 AD to 1798 AD which included the Dark Ages, the Crusaders and the Reformation. (Revelation 12:6)

34. Papal Rome received its deadly wound when Napoleon Bonaparte ordered Pope Pius Vl removal and took him to France, where he died a year later. This brought about the separation from both Church and State. The power of the State was returned into the Government's hand.

35. France. Between 1793 AD and 1798/9 AD during the reign of terror, the papacy suffered a great blow, about 17,000 clergy were killed, and the lands of the Catholic church were confiscated and returned into the hands of the state. Also their power over the state and church came to an end.

36. Sunday worship was introduced on 7th March 321 AD by Emperor Constantine 1 of Rome. This decree made Sunday a day of rest from labor, stating, "All Judges and City people and Craftsmen shall rest upon the venerable day of the sun."

37. Emperor Constantine 1.

38.

    a. Papal Rome.

    b. 1798 AD.

    c. France.

39. Daniel saw One like the Son of Man.

40. Jesus is the Son of Man.

41. The saints will possess the kingdom When Jesus returns to judge the ungodly.

42. The saints will possess the kingdom of heaven.

43. No. Jesus will not come back to live on this earth again. (1 Thessalonian 4:17).

44. Heaven and this earth shall pass away with fervent heat. (1 Thessalonian 4:17, Revelation 20:11)

45. The saints will be in the hands of this beast for a time, times and half a time, or 42 months or 1260 days. (remember a day in prophetic terms equals a year), (Daniel 7:25. Revelation 11:2, 12:6 & 14, Revelation 13:5} See (Numbers 14:34, and Ezekiel 4:5-6).

46. Time, times and half a time equal three and a half years, (but in prophetic terms a day equal to a year.) (also, the Jewish calendar carries 30 days in a month) therefore three and a half years are (3 times 12 months plus 6 months equal to 42 months times 30 days in a month equal 1260 days).

47. (Daniel 7:25), (Rev 11:2) (Rev 12:6) and (Rev 13:5).

a. (Daniel 7:25b) the holy people will be delivered into his hands for a time, times and half a time.

b. (Rev 11:2) But exclude the outer court; do not measure it, because it has been given to the Gentiles. They will trample on the holy city for 42 months.

c. Rev 12:6 The woman fled into the wilderness to a place prepared for her by God, where she might be taken care of for 1,260 days.

d. (Rev 13:5} The beast was given a mouth to utter proud words and blasphemies and to exercise its authority for forty-two months.

48. Jesus shall return under the rulers of those fourth kingdom on Earth in Daniel's vision. (Babylon, Mede & Persian, Greece, Rome and divided Rome). (Daniel 7:24-26}

49. The beast represents the nations with 10 horns and seven heads. (Rome and Divided Rome).

50. The 10 horns are:
    - Alemanni – Germany
    - Franks – French
    - Burgundians – Switzerland
    - Suevi – Portugal
    - Vandals - The Vandals were a Germanic Tribe that originated in Scandinavia and migrated across Europe
    - Visigoths – Spain
    - Anglo-Saxons – England
    - Ostrogoths - The Ostrogoths were a Germanic people who established the Ostrogothic Kingdom of Italy, which

controlled Italy and neighboring area from 493 AD to 553 AD

- Lombard – Italy
- Heruli - The Heruli are an Germanic people originally from Scandinavia

Seven heads are:

- Germany
- France
- Switzerland
- Portugal
- Spain
- England
- Italy

Bible Questions on Daniel's vision on the cleansing of the sanctuary

1. In the third year of King Belshazzar's reign Daniel had another vision. Where was Daniel at this time?
2. What did Daniel see at the beginning of this vision?
3. What was the description of the ram?
4. Which nation do the two horns on the ram represent?
5. The ram charged toward the west and north and south, which countries do they represent?
6. Who defeated the ram?
7. Which nation does the goat with the prominent horn represent?
8. What happened to the large prominent horn on the goat?
9. Who does this prominent horn on the goat represent?
10. Who do the four prominent horns on the goat that grew up later represent?
11. Where does the goat with the prominent horn between its eyes come from?
12. What happens to the goat at the height of its power?
13. How old was Alexander the Great when he died?
14. Out of one of the four horns that rule Greece came up another horn which started small but grew in power to the south and to the east and toward the Beautiful Land. Who was that horn?
15. Which nation threw some of the starry hosts down to the earth and trampled on them?

16. What did the Romans do to make themselves look like they were as great as the commander of the army of the LORD?
17. How long will it take for the vision to be fulfilled – the vision concerning the daily sacrifice, the rebellion that causes desolation, the surrender of the sanctuary and the trampling underfoot of the LORD's people?
18. Who informed Daniel what the meaning of his vision was all about?
19. When is this vision of Daniel going to be fulfilled?
20. How would this beast be destroyed?
21. Which angel will stand up during the end time and fight for God's people?
22. At this appointed time of the end, who will be delivered?
23. Which book do you think this is talking about?
24. What will happen to the multitudes who sleep in the dust of the earth when they awake?
25. What will happen to those who are wise?
26. What was Daniel told to do at the end of his vision?
27. What will many do during this time?
28. What did Daniel see after the end of his visions?
29. What did one of them say to the man clothed in linen, who was above the waters of the river?
30. What was the response of the man clothed in linen, who was above the waters of the river?

31. Did Daniel understand what he saw?
32. What was the response to Daniel when he asked, "My lord, what will the outcome of all this be, seeing he did not understand?"
33. Which horn will abolish the daily sacrifice, and set up the abomination that causes desolation?
34. How long will this time span be?
35. A blessing is awarded to the ones who wait for and reach the end of the 1,335 days. When is this?
36. When was this prophecy fulfilled?
    - When did the 1,290 days prophecy start?
    - When did it end?
37. Who was the ruler of France in 508 AD?
38. In what year did Clovis the first become king of France?
39. When did Clovis the first get married?
40. Who was Clovis the first's wife?
41. When did Clovis the first get converted to Catholicism?
42. In what year did Clovis the first get Baptiste?
43. By whom was Christianity spread in the Frankish kingdom?
44. What happened in France during the French revolution?
45. Who was the last king of France?
46. What is the name of King Clovis the First's dynasty?
47. Approximately how long did this dynasty survive?

48. What did France do to de-Christianize their nation?

49. How did France become a Republic State?

50. How was this carried out?

51. Why did France become de-Christianized?

52. When was the rejection of religion started in France?

53. The bible speaks of the two witnesses that tormented them. Who or what are these two witnesses?

54. The bible speaks about the dead bodies of these two witnesses which would lay in the streets of the city for three and a half days. When did this take place, and what is it talking about?

55. How long did this deChristianisation last?

56. When was the prophecy of the 1,335 days fulfilled?

57. The bible stated blessed is the one who waited and came to the 1,335 days. What are the blessings given to us who arrived after this date who live in the region of those 10 horns and seven heads in Daniel's prophecy?

58. How were we able to accomplish this freedom from God?

59. In what year were the 2,300 days, the 1,290 days and the 1,335 days prophecy fulfilled? (remember a day in prophetic terms equal 1 year) see (Numbers 14:34 and Ezekiel 4:5-6)?

60. Which sanctuary was re-consecrated in 1843/4?

61. Who is our sanctuary?

62. Who is our High Priest in our history today?

63. How do we know this?

64. Where in the bible does it state to us that Jesus is our sacrificial Lamb?

65. How do we show the world that we are spiritually cleansed and protected from the uncleanness of the world?

66. How do we know that Jesus is our sanctuary or Temple?

67. What are the items found in the tabernacle?

68. What is on the top of the mercy seat?

69. What or who do the cherubims represent?

70. How often was the priest able to enter the Holy of Holies?

71. What day would the priest enter the Holy of Holies?

72. What was put in the ark of the covenant?

73. When are the righteous, the children of God, being judged?

74. At what time does judgement begin in the church?

75. How do we know that judgement starts first with the children of God?

76. At what time will Jesus be setting-up his kingdom?

Answers to Bible questions on Daniel's vision of the cleansing of the sanctuary

1. In the Citadel of Susa in the Province of Elam, beside the Ulai Canal.
2. Before him was a ram with two horns standing beside the canal.
3. One of his horns was long, one of the horns was longer than the other, but grew up later.
4. Mede and Persian.
5.
   a. Lydia to the West.
   b. Babylon to the North.
   c. Egypt to the South.
   d. Goat.
6. Greece.
7. It was broken off, and four prominent horns grew in its place. (Daniel 11:3-4).
8. Alexander the Great.
9. Cassander, Ptolemy, Antigonus and Seleucus.
10. The West.
11. Its first ruler Alexander the Great died.
12. He was 33 years old (born July 356 BC and died June 323 BC)
13. Rome, came through Seleucus 1 Nicator, whose kingdom was the Seleucid Empire, one of the major powers of the Hellenistic World, which controlled most of Asia Minor, Syria, Mesopotamia

and the Iranian Plateau until it was overcome by the Roman Republic and Parthian Empire in the late Second and early First Centuries.

14. Rome.

15. The Roman general Titus invaded Jerusalem and destroyed the second temple in 70AD, they also looted the temple's sacred contents, including the golden table of shewbread, the seven-branded candlesticks, and a roll of the Law. The Romans paraded the temple treasures through the streets of Rome during Titus' triumphal procession. Most survivors were taken into slavery. The Romans also abolished the Sanhedrin and replaced it with the Roman procurator's Court. Many Jews left Judea to make their home elsewhere.

16. 2,300 evenings and mornings; then the sanctuary will be reconsecrated."

17. The angel Gabriel.

18. The vision concerns the appointed time of the End when Jesus will be returning to judge the ungodly.

19. By God, not by human hand.

20. The angel Michael.

21. Everyone whose name is found written in the book.

22. The Lamb's book of Life.

23. Some will wake to everlasting life, while others to shame and everlasting contempt.

24. They will shine like the brightness of the heavens, and those who lead many to righteousness will be like the stars for ever and ever.

25. To roll up and seal the words of the scroll until the time of the end.

26. Many will go here and there to increase their knowledge.

27. He sees two others standing before him, one on the bank of the river and one on the opposite bank.

28. "How long will it be before these astonishing things are fulfilled?"

29. He lifted his right hand and his left hand toward heaven and swore by him who lives forever, saying, "It will be for a time, times and half a time. when the power of the holy people has been completed."

30. No.

31. "Go your way, Daniel, because the words are rolled up and sealed until the time of the end. Many will be purified, made spotless and refined, but the wicked will continue to be wicked, none of the wicked will understand, but those who are wise will understand."

32. France.

33. The time span for this prophecy is 1,290 days. (In prophetic terms a day is equal to a year. See Numbers 14:34 and Ezekiel 4:5-6)

34. At the end of the 1,335 days (Remember a day is equal to a year).

35.
    a. Started 508/9 AD.
    b. Ended 1798/9 AD

36. King Clovis 1 of France.

37. In the year 481 AD.

38. In the year 493 AD when he was fifteen years old.

39. Clotilde who was a Catholic Christian.

40. In 496 AD.

41. In 508 AD.

42. King Clovis 1. He spread Christianity in the Frankish Kingdom (France and Germany) and the subsequent birth of the Holy Roman Empire.

43. The last King of France Louis XV1 and his wife Marie Antonette were executed for treason by the guillotine on 21st January 1793.

44. The last king of France is Louis XV1.

45. The Merovingian Dynasty.

46. About 200 years.

47. A statue of Liberty has replaced the Image of the "Blessed Virgin." The Mayor of Paris called this ceremony the "Festival of Liberty and Reason."
    The Insignia of the Catholic Religion in the church of Notre-Dame has been covered up, and a mound has been heaped up, on which stood a Greek Temple, with an inscription – 'To Philosophy' the 'Torch of Truth' flamed upon an altar. Young girls defiled (marched) in procession, they were clad in white, with tricolor sashes, and wore wreaths of flowers and carried torches. Then a beautiful woman, dressed in a mantle of blue and wearing the Red Cap. As the personification of Liberty, she received the homage of the Republicans, who stretched their hands towards her, and sang a hymn - "Come holy liberty, inhabit this Temple, become the Goddess of the French people.

48. By killing the last king of France Louis XV1, their last king, in the French Revolution.

49. This was carried out through the rebellion of the French people during the French Revolution.

50. They lost confidence in the Roman Catholic Church system and their monarchy.

51. 5th October 1793 and ended in 1798/9.

52. The Words of God, the Old and New Testament.

53. 21st January 1793 to 10th June 1796, during the Reign of Terror, The French nation de-Christianized the Church. They threw out God and the bible, and anything pertaining to the worship of God, and killed all those who proclaimed to be Christians, and threw out anything in their nation relating to religion.

54. Three and a half years. (The bible states for three and a half days their bodies lay in the street without burial). Remember a day represents a year in prophetic terms. (21st January 1793 to 10th June 1796)

55. In the year 1843/4.

56. We will be able to worship God freely, as we so wished. As the persecutions of worshipping God were now removed.

57. The bible was reintroduced into the churches, and because of the printed press many people could now purchase a bible and were able to read the words of God for themselves. Also, in our time of history the bible can be accessed in many different media devices. For instance, the Internet, YouTube, Facebook, Instagram and our phones.

58. In 1843/4 the beginning of the End of Time as we know it.
    - The 2,300 days started in 457 BC when King Artaxerxes of Persia made a decree to Ezra the priest to return to Jerusalem after their captivity by Nebuchadnezzar the

Babylonian to re-built Jerusalem. And ended in 1843/4 AD, our time in history.

- The 70 weeks or (Seventy 'Seven') prophecy. (490 years in prophetic terms.) Started in 457 BC and ended approximately 36 AD.
- The 1,260 days or time, times and half a time, (3 ½ years) or 42 months started in 538 ADS when Papal Rome began its reign and ended in 1798 AD during the Reign of Terror.
- The 1,335 days started in 508 ADS when King Clovis 1 got baptized and helped to Christianize the Germanic nations under the Roman Catholic Church in 509 AD and ended in 1843/4 AD. The time when the sanctuary was re-consecrated.

59. The Sanctuary in Heaven.

60. Our Redeemer the Lord Jesus Christ. (Hebrews 8:1-2 and Psalm 90:1)

61. Jesus Christ the Son of God.

62. See Hebrew 4:14-16
Therefore, since we have a great High Priest who has ascended into heaven, Jesus the Son of God, let us hold firmly to the faith we profess. For we do not have a High Priest who is unable to empathize with our weaknesses, but we have one who has been tempted in every way, just as we are – yet he did not sin. Let us then approach God's throne of grace with confidence, so that we may receive mercy and grace to help us in our time of need.

63. John 1:29 and John 1:36
The next day John saw Jesus coming toward him and said, "Look, the Lamb of God, who takes away the sin of the world! When he saw Jesus passing by, he said, "Look, the Lamb of God!"

64. Through water baptism, showing the world by displaying His character, (the fruit of the spirit, Galatians 5:22-23). Showing we accepted Jesus Christ as our Savior.

65. I did not see a temple in the city, because the Lord God Almighty and the Lamb are its Temple. (Revelation 21:22).

66. The Table of Shewbread, the Candlestick, the Altar of Incense, and the Ark of the Covenant.

67. Two Cherubims.

68. The Angels.

69. Once a year.

70. The day of Atonement.

71. The book of the law - the Ten Commandments, Aaron's rod that budded and Manna.

72. Starting from the re-Consecration of the Sanctuary, the end of the 2,300 evenings and mornings, (from 1843/4 AD until the time of Jesus returns.)

73. Right after the re-Consecration of the Temple.

74. For it is time for judgement to begin with God's household; and if it begins with us, what will the outcome be for those who do not obey the gospel of God? And "If it is hard for the righteous to be saved, what will become of the ungodly and the sinner?" So then, those who suffer according to God's will, should commit themselves to their faithful Creator and continue to do good. (1 Peter 4:17-19).

75. At the end of the fulfillment of those beasts, (Babylon, Mede & Persian, Greece, Rome and divided Rome), Jesus will be setting-up his kingdom. (Daniel 2:35, 44-45).

Bible Questions on St Matthew Chapter 24

1. What are the three questions the disciples asked Jesus on the mount of Olives?
2. What were Jesus' disciples drawing His attention to, when they were on the Mount of Olives?
3. What was Jesus's response to them?
4. Did this prophecy of Jesus come true?
5. When in our history did this come to pass?
6. What was Jesus warning the Jews to be aware of?
7. What were they told not to do?
8. Why do you think they were given this warning?
9. Were pregnant women and nursing mothers given warning?
10. What would happen to pregnant women and nursing mothers?
11. Why were they told to pray that their flight would not be on the Sabbath or in winter?
12. What were they told about how dreadful that time would be?
13. Why did Jesus' cry over Jerusalem?
14. Which nation did God use to carry out this prophetic fulfilment?
15. What did the Romans do to Jerusalem?
16. How was the temple destroyed?
17. What did Jesus call this time in history?
18. Will this ever happen again in our world history?

19. How do we know it will never happen again?
20. Why were so many Jews not prepared in Jerusalem in 70 AD?
21. Approximately how many Jews were enslaved?
22. What was Jesus' warning to His people?
23. Why was Jesus giving this warning?
24. What are the signs Jesus warns us to look out for?
25. What will happen after all the things in question 24 are fulfilled?
26. Have we seen in our history any of those things fulfilled?
27. If yes, what are examples of some of the fulfilment of these things?
28. What is the reason Jesus gives for his saints being persecuted?
29. Why didn't Jesus warn his disciples beforehand about what was going to happen at the end of time?
30. What will God do for His elect's sake?
31. What would have happened if time was not shortened?
32. Why did Jesus warn his disciple to look out for deceivers?
33. Would the false Prophets and false Christ be able to deceive the elect?
34. What is it we should not believe if anyone told us that Christ has come?
35. Why should we not believe anyone who tells us Christ is in a particular location?
36. What will happen immediately after the distress of those days when Jesus would be returning?

37. Why will the people living at this appointed time be mourning?
38. What command will Jesus give to his angels at this appointed time at the end of the age?
39. What is the parable Jesus says that the people living this time in earth history must learn?
40. Why were we given this parable?
41. Which generation will not pass until all is fulfilled?
42. What will pass away before any of God's words pass away?
43. Does anyone know the time when Jesus will be returning?
44. How do we know that no one knows the time or hour when Jesus will be returning?
45. Does this mean Jesus does not know when he will be returning to judge the living and the dead?
46. How many parables did Jesus tell his disciples relating to His kingdom and the end of the age?
47. Can you name the parables?
48. Why will the ungodly be weeping and gnashing their teeth?
49. What will happen to the unbelievers at Jesus coming?
50. Where in the Bible do you find that the birds of the sky will eat up the flesh of the unbelievers?
51. What punishment awaits the ungodly?
52. What awaits the believers?
53. What rewards will God be giving His saints?

Answers to Bible Questions on St Matthew Chapter 24

1.
    a. "Tell us," They said, "When will this happen?
    b. And what shall be the sign of your coming?
    c. And at the end of the age?

2. The beauty of the temple.

3. He says to them, "Do you see all these things? Truly I tell you, not one stone here will be left on another; everyone will be thrown down."

4. Yes.

5. 70 AD (Deuteronomy 28:49-50).

6. 'The abomination that causes desolation,' spoken of by the prophet Daniel. (Leviticus 26:29-33, Deuteronomy 28:48-68).

7. Those who are in Judea flee to the mountains. Let no-one on the roof of the house go down to take anything out of the house. Let no-one in the field go back to take his cloak.

8. Their enemies, the Romans, were going to surround them on every side. (Deuteronomy 28:52, Luke 19:42-44, Luke 21:20-22).

9. Yes, they were warned that at the given time of fulfilment it would be very dreadful for them.

10. They were going to eat their after birth, their children and each other in the siege because of the famine in the land and the war. See (Deuteronomy 28:53 & 57).

11. They will not be able to flee. They would be trapped on the Sabbath as they're locked in within their gate. They are also not

supposed to do anything apart from worship on the Sabbath. In the winter it would be very hard to flee or hide in the cold weather.

12. They would be under great distress, unequaled from the beginning of the world until then – and never to be equalled again (Deuteronomy 28:48-67).

13. Jesus cried over Jerusalem because he knew His people were going to reject Him, and the prince of this world who is the Devil would come, and he was going to destroy them, for they didn't know the time of their visitation.

14. The Romans.

15. They built a trench around it and ebbed in the people on every side. They let people enter the city but let no-one out. Many Jews that were killed were visitors who came from all over the world for the Passover festival.

16. They broke down the temple of Jerusalem layer by layer so as not to damage the precious stones the temple was built with. Therefore, they were not left one stone upon another as Jesus predicted.

17. The Time of Great Tribulation for the Jews.

18. No, what happened to the Jews during the great tribulation will never happen again.

19. Matthew 24:21 states, for then they will be in great distress, unequaled from the beginning of the world until then – and never to be equal again.

20. Many people were attending the Jewish yearly Passover Festival. It was only three days before the festival, so many Jews would already arrive in Jerusalem for the Passover.

21. According to historians about 97,000 Jews were enslaved.

22. Let no one deceive you.

23. He knew many would come under the disguise, and say they are God, and they shall deceive many.

24.
   a. Wars and rumors of wars
   b. Nation rising against Nation and Kingdom against Kingdom.
   c. Famines and Earthquakes in various places.
   d. Persecutions and Death for God's children, because of their faith in Jesus.
   e. Many believers will turn away from the faith and betray and hate each other.
   f. Many false prophets will appear and deceive many.
   g. Wickedness will increase, and the love of many will grow cold.
   h. This gospel of the kingdom will be preached in all the world as a testimony to all nations.

25. The end will then come.

26. Yes.

27.
   a. Wars:
   1914- 1918 World War 1, 22 million died.
   1915 The Armenian genocide, over 1 million victims.
   1933 Nazis came into power, over 6 million Jews killed in the Holocaust.

World War 2, over 60 million died.
1947 - 1991 Cold War, started at the end of World War 2 and ended 26th December 1991 at the dissolution of the Soviet Union.
1950-1953 Korean War, over 5 million died.
1964-1975 Vietnam War, over 3 million died.
1991 The Gulf War – bombing raid on Iraq, over 600,000 deaths.
There have been many more wars all over the world before and since then, for i.e. Russia and Kuwait and Israel and Palestinian.

b. b. Earthquakes:
Nov 1755 The Great Lisbon Earthquake.
1989 – Loma Prieta Earthquake in San Francisco Bay area, California, U.S.A. Hurricane Hugo across the Northeastern Caribbean and Southeastern United States.
There have been many more Earthquakes all around the world. Earthquakes are now occurring across the world every day.

c. c. Famines:
1315 - 1317 The Great Famine of Europe.
1601 – 1603 The worst Famine in Russia.
1630 – 1632 The Famine of Deccan Plateau in India.
1740 – 1741 The Irish Famine (Greater lost than 1845-1852).
1768 – 1773 The Great Bengal Famine.
1845 – 1852 The second Irish Famine.
1891 – 1892 The Great Famine of Russia.
1917 – 1919 The Great Famine of Persia.
1959 – 1961 The Great Famine of China.
There have been many more famines before and after around the world.
Persecution of God's people all around the world. (Acts 9:1 up until present day.)

28. The persecutors do not know God the Father or me, Jesus.

29. Jesus' mission with them was coming to an end, and He was now preparing to leave.

30. He shortens the time.

31. No-one would survive.

32. False Christ and false prophets would appear and would perform great signs and miracles to deceive the very elect.

33. No.

34. If anyone tells us, "There He is or that He is in the desert," do not go out, or "Here He is, in the inner rooms," do not believe it.

35. As lighting that comes from the east is visible even in the west, so will be the coming of the Son of Man. Those who are living at that appointed time will all know at the same time.

36. "The sun will be darkened, and the moon will not give its light, the stars will fall from the sky, and the heavenly body will be shaken."

37. They shall see the sign of the Son of Man coming in the clouds of the sky, with power and great glory, and they are not ready for His return.

38. He shall send his angels with a loud trumpet call, and they shall gather the elect from the four winds, from the one end of heaven to the other. (1 Thessalonian 4:16)

39. Now learn the parable of the fig tree: As soon as its twigs get tender and leaves come out, you know that summer is near.

40. For them to understand that His coming is near, even at the door.

41. This question had a double meaning. It refers to the generation living during that time of the Great Tribulation, 70 AD. And those living at the end of time.

42. Heaven and Earth as we know it.

43. No.

44. Matthew 24:36 "But about the day and the hour no one knows, not even the angels in heaven, nor the Son, but the Father only."

45. When Jesus was in His humanity it is possible it was not yet revealed to Him, but now after His death, burial and resurrection, and now that He has taken back His Divinity, He does know. In the bible we are told by Jesus that He and the Father are one. While He was here on earth, He told us He only did what His Father told Him. (John 5:19: "Jesus says,'The Son can do nothing of his own accord, but only what he sees the Father doing'". And John 12:49-50: "Jesus says, 'I didn't come to reject the world; I came to save the world. But you need to know that whoever puts me off, refusing to take in what I'm saying, is willfully choosing rejection. The Father who sent me gave me orders, told me what to say and how to say it.'"

46. Jesus talked about nine parables pertaining to His kingdom and the end of the age.

47.

   a. The wheat and weeds (Matthew 13:36-42).

   b. The 10 virgins, five were wise and five were foolish (Matthew 25:1-10).

   c. A net let down into the lake to catch fish, and then separate the good from the bad (Matthew 13:47-30).

   d. The fig tree (Matthew 24:32-33).

e. The kingdom of heaven is like a man sowing good seeds into his field, and the enemy came and sowed bad seeds among them (Matthew 13:24-30).

f. Noah's Ark (Matthew 24:37-39).

g. Two men in a field, the one will be taken and the other left (Matthew 24:40).

h. Two women will be grinding with a hand mill; the one will be taken and the other left (Matthew 24:41).

i. The wicked servant (Matthew 24:48-51).

48. They will be weeping and gnashing their teeth, when those ungodly ones see how the evil one has deceived them; and cause them to lose out on eternal life.

49. They all will die from the brightness of Jesus' countenance. And the foul of the air will eat up their flesh.

50. Revelation 19:17-19 says, "And I saw an angel standing in the sun, who cried in a loud voice to all the birds flying in midair, 'Come. Gather for the great supper of God, so that you may eat the flesh of kings, generals, and the mighty, of horses and their riders, and the flesh of all people, free and slave, great and small.'"

51. The second death. Total and final separation from God.

52. A home in New Jerusalem, which will be coming down from heaven.

53. They will receive a crown of life and will live eternally with the Father. They will not cry anymore, for God will wipe away all tears from their eyes. There will be no more mourning, death, or pains, for the old order of things will be passed away. We will be like angels in heaven. See (Daniel 10:5-6)

"I lifted my eyes and looked and there before me was a man dressed in linen, with a belt of the finest gold round his waist. His body was like chrysolite, his face like lighting, his eyes like flaming torches, his arms and legs like the gleam of burnished bronze, and his voice like the sound of a multitude."

This is what we will be like when we change from mortality to immortality in a twinkling of an eye.

APPENDIX II

THE KINGS AND QUEENS OF ISRAEL

NAME:	D.O.B	REIGN	DIED	REASONS:
Saul	1078 Bc	1050 - 1010 Bc	1010 Bc	Was 28 Years Old When He Began To Reign, And He Reigned 40 Years. He Killed Himself In Battle By Falling On His Sword.
David	1040 Bc	1010 - 970 Bc	970 Bc	Was 39 Years Old When He Began To Reign, And He Reigned For 40 Years In Israel, For 7 Years In Hebron, And 33 Years In *Jerusalem (1 Kings 2: 11).*
Solomon	990 Bc	971 - 931 Bc	931 Bc	Was 19 Years Old When He Began To Reign, And Reigned For 40 Years In Israel *(1 Kings 11: 42).*

NAME:	D.O.B	REIGN	DIED	REASONS:
Jeroboam 1		931 - 910 Bc	910 Bc	He Set Up Golden Calves In Bethel And The City Of Dan For The People To Worship, And Also Appointed Priests From All Sort Of People, Even Though They Were Not Levites. Through Him God's Entire System Of Holy Days Sacrifices And Worship Was Changed
Nabad		910 - 909 Bc	909 Bc	Reigned For 2 Years, He Followed In The Footstep Of His Wicked Father Jeroboam And Led Israel Into Deeper Sin. He Was Assassinated. Co-Regent With Jeroboam. *(1 Kings 15:25 & 28.)*
Baasha		909 - 886 Bc	886 Bc	Reigned For 24 Years, He Was An Evil Ruler. He Killed All Of Jeroboam's Family And Followed Idolatrous Practices. *(1 Kings 15:33)*.

NAME:	D.O.B	REIGN	DIED	REASONS:
Elah		886 - 885 Bc	885 Bc	He Reigned For 2 Years, And Was Co-Regent With Baasha, Zimri, Tibni And Omri. He Was Killed By Zimri And All His Household Was Killed With Him. (1 Kings 16: 8 & 1 Kings 16: 10).
Zimri		884 Bc	884 Bc	His Reign Lasted 7 Days. He Did Evil In The Sight Of The Lord. He Killed All The Household Of Baasha, He Set The Royal Palace On Fire And Died In The Fire. (1 Kings 16:11 & 1 Kings 16:15 & 18).
Tibni		884 - 880 Bc	880 Bc	Reigned For 4 Years, Co-Regent With Omri. *(1 Kings 16: 22)*
Omri		884 - 873 Bc	873 Bc	He Reigned For 12 Years, And Did Evil In The Sight Of The Lord - He Did Worse Than All Who Were Before Him. *(1 Kings 16:16 & 1 Kings 16:23)*
		884 - 880 Bc		Co-Regent With Tibni
		881 - 874 Bc		Sole Reign
		874 - 873 Bc		Co-Regent With Ahab

NAME:	D.O.B	REIGN	DIED	REASONS:
Ahab		874 - 852 Bc	852 Bc	He Reigned For 22 Years Over Israel In Samaria, And He Also Did Evil In The Sight Of The Lord Above All Those Who Were Before Him. He Set Up An Altar For Baal In The House Of Baal Which He Built In Samaria. *(1 Kings 16:29).*
		874 - 873 Bc		Co- Regent With Omri
		873 - 852 Bc		Sole Reign
Ahaziah Of Israel	875 Bc	853 - 852 Bc	852 Bc	He Was 22 Year Old When He Began To Reign, And Reign 2 Years
		853 - 852 Bc		Co-Regent With Ahab
Jehoram (Joram)	870 Bc	853- 840 Bc	840 Bc	He Was 17 Years Old When He Began To Reign, And Reigned For 12 Years. He Did Evil In The Sight Of The Lord, But Not Like His Father And Mother, For He Put Away The Image Of Baal That His Father Made. *(2 Kings 1:17).*

NAME:	D.O.B	REIGN	DIED	REASONS:
Jehu	882 Bc	841 - 814 Bc	814 Bc	He Was 41 Years Old When He Began To Reign, And Reigned For 28 Years In Samaria, Exterminating The House Of Ahab. He Did Evil In The Eyes Of The Lord. Because Of The Evil He Did, His Children Would Rule Only To Their Fourth Generation *(2 Kings 10:36).*
Jehoahaz		814 - 797 Bc	797 Bc	He Reigned For 17 Years, And He Did What Was Evil In The Sight Of The Lord. (2 Kings 13:1).
Jehoash King Of Israel		798 - 782 Bc	782 Bc	He Reigned For 16 Years, And He Did Evil In The Sight Of The Lord. *(2 Kings 13:10).*
		798 - 797 Bc		Co-Regent With Jehoahaz
		797 - 782 Bc		Sole Reign
Jeroboam 11		781 - 740 Bc	740 Bc	He Reigned For 41 Years, And He Did That Which Was Evil In The Sight Of The Lord. There Was A Large Earthquake In 760 Bc, During The Latter Part Of His Reign. *(2 Kings 14:23).*

NAME:	D.O.B	REIGN	DIED	REASONS:
		781 - 782 Bc		Co-Regent With Jehoash
		782 - 740 Bc		Sole Reign
Zechariah		752 Bc	752 Bc	He Reigned For 6 Months, And He Did What Was Evil In The Sight Of The Lord. He Was Killed By Shallum The Son Of Jabesh. *(2 Kings 15:8).*
		752 Bc		Co-Regent With Jeroboam 11
Shallum		753 Bc	753 Bc	He Reigned For One Month, And Was Killed By Menahem. This Period Was The Fulfilment Of The Lord To Jehu, Saying Thy Sons Shall Sit On The Throne Of Israel To The 4th Generation. *(2 Kings 15:13).*
		753 Bc		Co-Regent With Jeroboam 11
Menahem		753 - 743 Bc	743 Bc	He Reigned For 10 Years In Samaria, And He Did That Which Was Evil In The Sight Of The Lord. He Killed Shallum, And Ripped Up All The Women That Were With Child In Tiphsah .*(2 Kings 15:17).*
		753 - 743 Bc		Co-Regent With Jeroboam 11

NAME:	D.O.B	REIGN	DIED	REASONS:
Pekahiah		742 - 740 Bc	740 Bc	He Reigned For 2 Years, Was Co-Regent With Menahem And Pekah, And He Continued The Sin Of Jeroboam And Was Assassinated By Pekah. *(2 Kings 15:23).*
		740 - 742 Bc		Co-Regent With Jeroboam 11
Pekah		740 - 720 Bc	720 Bc	He Reigned For 20 Years, And He Did That Was Evil In The Sight Of The Lord. He Was Killed By Hoshea. (2 Kings 15:27).
Hoshea		732 - 723 Bc	Went Into Capti vity	He Reigned For 9 Years, And Was Taken Into Captivity To Assyria By Shalmaneser. In The Seventh Year Of Hoshea, Shalmaneser King Of Assyria Came Up Against Samaria, And Besieged It, And At The End Of Three Years They Took It Even In The Sixth Year Of Hezekiah , Which Was The Ninth Year Of Hoshea King Of Israel. *(2 Kings 18:9-10).*

THE KINGS AND QUEENS OF JUDAH

NAME:	D.O.B	REIGN	DIED	REASONS:
Rehoboam	972 Bc	931 - 915/914 Bc	915/914 Bc	He Was 41 Years Old When He Began To Reign, And Reigned 17 Years In Jerusalem. He Caused Judah To Sin By Building High Places And Images And Groves, On Every High Hill, And Under Every Green Tree. They Also Had Sodomites In The Land. *(1 Kings 14: 21 & 2 Chronicles 9:30).*
Abijah	950 Bc	914/913 - 911 Bc	911 Bc	He Reigned For 3 Years In Jerusalem, And He Walked In The Sins Of His Father. *(1 Kings 15: 1-2 7 2 Chronicles 13:1).*
Asa	932 B	911 - 870 Bc	870 Bc	He Was 21 Year Old When He Began To Reign, Was The Third King Of The Southern Kingdom And He Reigned For 41 Years. He Did What Was Right, But He Was Diseased In His Feet In The 29th Year Of His Reign, But Didn't Seek The Lord, Instead Sought Help From Physicians. *(1 Kings 15: 9-10 & 2 Chronicles 16:12 -13).*

NAME:	**D.O.B**	**REIGN**	**DIED**	**REASONS:**
Jehoshaphat	907 Bc	874 - 849 Bc	849 Bc	He Was 33 Years Old When He Began To Reign, And Reigned For 25 Years. He Did What Was Right In The Sight Of The Lord. *(1 Kings 22:41 -42 & 2 Chronicles 20:31).*
		874 - 870 Bc		Co-Regent With Asa
		870 - 849 Bc		Sole Reign
Jehoram	882 Bc	850 - 842 Bc	842 Bc	He Was 32 Years Old When He Began To Reign, And Reigned For 8 Years. He Killed All His Brothers, And He Was Killed By Jehu.
		850 - 849 Bc		Co-Regency With His Father Jehoshaphat
		849 - 842 Bc		Sole Reign
Ahaziah (Jehoahaz 1)	864 Bc	842 - 841 Bc	841 Bc	He Was 22 Years Old When He Began His Reign, And Reigned For One Year. He Deliberately Led The People Away From God While He Was In Power. *(2 Kings 8:25 - 26 & 2 Kings 9:29 & Chronicle 22:2).* *2 Chronicles 22 Says He Was*

NAME:	D.O.B	REIGN	DIED	REASONS:
				Forty Two Years Old When He Began To Reign, And Was Co-Regent With Jehoram
Athaliah	898 Bc	841 - 835 Bc	835 Bc	She Reigned For Seven Years, Was The Daughter Of Ahaz And Queen Jezebel, And Killed All The Seed Royal Apart From Joash Whom Jehosheba Stole And Hid In The House Of The Lord For Six Years. *(2 Kings 11:1-2 & 2 Chronicles 22:12 & 15).*
Joash (Jehoash)	843 Bc	836 - 796 Bc	796 Bc	He Started His Reign At Age Seven, Reigned For 40 Years And Did What Was Right In The Sight Of The Lord. After The Death Of Jehoiada, He Caused The Death Of Zechariah The Son Of Jehoiada The Priest. He Was Killed In The House Of Millo. *(2 Kings 12:1 - 2 & 20, 2 Chronicle 24:1 & 20 - 22).*
		836 - 835 Bc		Co-Regent With Athaliah
		836 - 796 Bc		Sole Reign

NAME:	D.O.B	REIGN	DIED	REASONS:
Amaziah	821 Bc	796 - 767 Bc	767 Bc	He Was 25 Years Old When He Began To Reign, And Reigned For 29 Years. He Did That Which Was Right In The Sight Of The Lord, But Not With A Perfect Heart. He Slew His Servant Who Had Killed His Father. *(2 Kings 14: 1-2 & 2 Chronicles 25:1).*
		796 - 785 Bc		Sole Reign
		785 - 767 Bc		Co-Regency With His Son Uzziah
Uzziah (Azariah)	808 Bc	792 - 740 Bc	740 Bc	He Was 16 Years Old When He Began To Reign, And Reigned For 52 Years. He Did What Was Right In The Sight Of The Lord, Was Struck With Leprosy For Disobeying The Lord, And By Burning Incense In The Temple, Because This Must Be Done Only By Priests. *(2 Kings 15:1-2 & 2 Chronicles 26:1 - 3).*
		792 - 767 Bc		Co-Regency With His Father Amaziah
		767 - 751 Bc		Sole Reign
		751 - 740 Bc		Co-Regency With His Son Jotham

NAME:	D.O.B	REIGN	DIED	REASONS:
Jotham	763 Bc	738 - 722 Bc	722 Bc	He Was 25 Years Old When He Began To Reign, And Reigned For 16 Years. He Did What Was Right In The Sight Of The Lord. *(2 Kings 15:32 & 2 Chronicles 27:1 & 8).*
Ahaz	743 Bc	723 - 707 Bc	707 Bc	He Was 20 Years Old When He Began To Reign, And Reigned For 16 Years In Jerusalem. He Did What Was Evil In The Sight Of The Lord, And He Made His Son To Pass Through The Fire According To The Abomination Of The Heathen. *(2 Kings 16:1-2 & 2 Chronicles 28:1).*
		723 - 722 Bc		Co-Regent With Jotham
		723 - 707 Bc		Sole Reign
Hezekiah	741 Bc	716- 687 Bc	687 Bc	He Was 25 Years Old When He Began To Reign, And Reigned For 29 Years In Jerusalem. He Did That Which Was Right In The Sight Of The Lord.(2 Kings 18:1-2 & 2 Chronicles 29:1).
		716 - 707 Bc		Co-Regent With Ahaz
		706 - 687 Bc		Sole Reign

NAME:	D.O.B	REIGN	DIED	REASONS:
Manasseh	699 Bc	687 - 632 Bc	632 Bc	He Was 12 Years Old When He Began To Reign, And Reigned For 55 Years. He Did Evil In The Sight Of The Lord, But Was Forgiven After He Humbled Himself Before The Lord. *(2 Kings 21:1 & 2 Chronicles 33:1).*
Amon	664 Bc	642 - 641 Bc	641 Bc	He Was 22 Years Old When He Began To Reign, And Reigned For 2 Years, And Did Evil In The Sight Of The Lord, Until He Was Assassinated. *(2 Kings 21:19 & 2 Chronicles 33:21).*
		642 - 641 Bc		Co-Regent With Manasseh
Josiah	648 Bc	640 - 609 Bc	609 Bc	He Began To Reign At The Age Of 8 Years, And Reigned For 31 Years. He Did That Which Was Right In The Sight Of God *(See 2 Kings 22:1 & 2 Chronicles 34:1).*
Jehoahaz 111	632 Bc	609 Bc	Taken Into Capti vity	He Was 23 Years Old When He Began To Reign, And Reigned For Three Months In Jerusalem. He Did Evil In The Sight Of The Lord, According To All That His Fathers Has Done. He Was

NAME:	D.O.B	REIGN	DIED	REASONS:
				Taken To Egypt And Put In Bands By Pharaoh-Necho. *(2 Kings 23:31 & 2 Chronicles 36:2).*
Eliakim (Jehoiakim)	634 Bc	609 - 598 Bc	598 Bc	He Was 25 Years Old When He Began To Reign, And He Reigned For 11 Years In Jerusalem, And He Did Evil In The Sight Of The Lord According To All That His Father Has Done. *(2 Kings 23:36 & 2 Chronicles 36:5).*
Jehoiachin	615 Bc	598 - 597 Bc	Went Into Capti vity	He Was 18 Years Old When He Began To Reign, And Reigned For 3 Months From 9th Dec 598 - 15/16 March 597 Bc, When He Was Dethroned By Nebuchadnezzar And Taken Into Captivity, Along With His Household, And All The Treasures Of The House Of The Lord. 'and The Treasures Of The King's House, And Cut In Pieces All The Vessels Of Gold Which Solomon King Of Israel Had Made In The Temple Of The Lord, As The Lord Has Said. And He Carried Away All Jerusalem, And All The Princes, And All

NAME:	D.O.B	REIGN	DIED	REASONS:
				The Mighty Men Of Valour, Even All The Craftsmen And Smiths: None Remained, Save The Poorest Sort Of People Of The Land' *2 Kings 24:11-16. & 2 Chronicles 36:9,* In *2 Chronicles 36:9* It Stated He Was 8 Years Old When He Began To Reign. I Think This Is An Error.
Zedekiah (Mattaniah)	618 Bc	597 - 586 Bc	Went Into Capti vity	He Was 21 Years Old When He Began To Reign, And Reigned For 11 Years. He Did Evil In The Sight Of The Lord And Would Not Humble Himself, And So He Was Taken Into Captivity, And His Sons Were Killed Before His Eyes. His Eyes Were Plucked Out And He Was Bound With Fetters Of Brass, And Taken To Babylon, Where He Died. 'for Through The Anger Of The Lord It Came To Pass In Jerusalem And Judah, Until He Had Cast Them Out From His Presence, That Zedekiah Rebelled Against The King Of Babylon.' He Is The Last King Of Judah. *2 Kings 24: 18 - 20 & 2 Chronicles 36:11*

REIGNING KINGS AND QUEENS IN THE BIBLE

Babylonian Kings

NAME:	D.O.B	REIGN	DIED	REASONS:
Nebuchadnezzar	630bc	605 -562 Bc	562 Bc	He Reigned For 43 Years. In The 8th Year Of His Reign King Nebuchadnezzar Took Jehoiachin, All Of His Household, The Princes, All The Mighty Men, All The Craftsmen And Smiths, And All The Treasuries Of The House Of The Lord And The King. *(2 Kings 24:10-16).*
Amel-Marduk (Evil-Merodach)		562 - 560 Bc	560 Bc	He Reigned For 2 Years, And Was Assassinated On 27th December 560 Bc. In The Year He Began To Reign He Lifted Up The Head Of King Jehoiachin, And Brought Him Out Of Prison And Changed His Prison Garments, And Talked Kindly To Him, And Set Him Up Above The Kings Of Babylon, And Gave Him A Daily Allowance For All The Rest Of His Life. *(See 2 Kings 25:27 -30 And Jeremiah 52:31-34).*
		562 Bc		Co-Regent With Nebuchadnezzar
		561 -560 Bc		Sole Reign
		560 Bc		Co-Regent With Neriglissar
Neriglissar (Nergal-Sharezer)		Aug 560 - Apr 556 Bc	Apr 556 Bc	He Reigned For 3 Years And 8 Months
Labashi-Marduk		Apr 556 - Jun 556 Bc	June 556 Bc	He Reigned For 9 Months, And He Was An Evil King
Nebonidos	615 Bc	556 - 539 Bc	539 Bc	Was Taken Into Exile By The Persians 539 Bc
Belshazzar	580 Bc	546 - 539 Bc	539 Bc	He Shared Part Of His Reign With Nebonidos, And He Was Killed By The Persians

Median & Persian Kings

NAME:	D.O.B	REIGN	DIED	REASONS:
Cyaxares 11 (Darius)	599 Bc	539 - 537 Bc	537 Bc	He Reigned For 2 Years , And He Died Of Old Age
Cyrus The Great King Of Medes/Persia	590 Bc	559 - 530 Bc	530 Bc	He Reigned For 7 Years Over Babylon From 537 - 530 Bc. 'now In The First Year Of Cyrus The King Of Persia, The Children Of Judah And Benjamin Were Returned To Jerusalem, To Rebuilt The Temple The House Of The Lord.' *(Ezra 4:1-5).*
		Conquered Babylon 539 Bc		
Cambeesee 11	559 Bc	530 - 522 Bc	522 Bc	Reign 8 Years, Left Egypt To Deal With Rebellion In Persia, He Sustained A Wound To The Thigh, Which Got Infected With Gangrene, He Died 3 Weeks Later.
Darius The Great (Darius 1)	550 Bc	522 - 486 Bc	486 Bc	He Reigned For 36 Years, And He Was 64 Years When He Died. Ezra 6, Darius Made A Decree For The Children Of Judah And Benjamin To Start Back The Rebuilding Of The Temple , And Anyone Who Altered This Decree, Let The Timber Of His House Be Pulled Down, And Being Set Up, Let Him Be Hanged Thereon; And Let His House Be Made A Dunghill For This. In Their Way. The Temple, The House Of The Lord Was Finished And Built In The Third Day Of The Month Adar, In The Sixth Year Of The Reign Of Darius.

NAME:	D.O.B	REIGN	DIED	REASONS:
Xerxes 1 (Ahasuerus)	519 Bc	Oct 486 - 465 Bc	11th Aug 465 Bc	He Reigned For 21 Years, And Then Was Assassinated
Artaxerxes 1	518 Bc	Aug 465 - 424 Bc	424 Bc	He Reigned For 41 Years, And Was 94 Years Old When He Died. During The Early Part Of The Reign Of King Artaxerxes 1, The Adversaries Of The Children Of Judah And Benjamin Wrote A Letter Complaining About Them, Accusing Them Of Trouble Making To Stop Them From Building The House Of God *(Ezra 4:7-20).* They Were Given The Command To Let The Work Cease Until Another Command Was Given By Him. *(Ezra 4:21).* In The Seventh Year Of His Reign, Artaxerxes Made A Decree Giving Ezra And The People Of Israel And The Priests And Levites Who Wanted To Of Their Own Free Will, To Be Able To Go Up To Jerusalem And Rebuild It. *(Ezra 7:13-38).*
Xerxes 11		425 - 424 Bc	424 Bc	He Reigned For 45 Days, And Then Was Assassinated
Sogdianus		424 - 423 Bc	423 Bc	He Reigned For 6 Months. And Then Was Assassinated
Darius 11 (Ezra 6)	475 Bc	423 - 404 Bc	404 Bc	He Reigned For 19 Years, And Was 71 Years When He Died. *(Ezra 7).*
Artaxerxes 11	453 Or 445 Bc	404 - 358 Bc	358 Bc	He Reigned For 46 Years, And Died At The Age Of 86 Or 94

NAME:	D.O.B	REIGN	DIED	REASONS:
Artaxerxes 111	425 Bc	358 - 338 Bc	338 Bc	He Reigned For 20 Years, And Died At The Age 87 When He Was Assassinated
Arses		338 - 336 Bc	336 Bc	He Reigned For 2 Years, And Then He Was Poisoned By Eunuch Bagoas.
Darius 111	381 Bc	336 - 330 Bc	July 330 Bc Bactria	Darius 111 Was Killed By His Cousin During The Take Over Of Persia By Alexander The Great, And He Was The Last Of The Achaemenid Dynasty
Daniel	612 Bc		528 Bc	He Went Into Captivity Around 597 Bc. He Died At The Age Of 84 Years

Kings of Ancient Greece

NAME:	D.O.B	REIGN	DIED	REASONS:
Alexander 111 Of Macedon (The Great)	356 Bc	336 Bc - 323 Bc	323 Bc	He Reigned For 13 Years, And Died At The Age Of 33 Years
Antipater	400 Bc	323 - 319 Bc	**319 Bc**	One Of The Generals Taken Over After The Death Of Alexander
Perdiccas	365 Bc	323 - 321 Bc	**321 Bc**	One Of The Generals Taken Over After The Death Of Alexander The Great, He Was Murdered By His Officer (Peithon Antigens, And Seleucus) His Officers And The Rest Of His Army Defected To Ptolemy.
Ptolemy 1 Sotor	367 Bc	305/04 - 283 Bc	**283 Bc**	He Was A Companion And Historian Of Alexander The Great Of The Kingdom Of Macedon In Northern Greece

NAME:	D.O.B	REIGN	DIED	REASONS:
				Who Became Ruler Of Egypt, And Was Part Of Alexander's Former Empire.
Seleucus 1 Nicator	358 Bc	306 -281 Bc	281 Bc	He Was Co-King With Antiochus 1 Soter, And Was Assassinated September 281, At The Age Of 77 Years
Antiochus 1 Soter	324/3 Bc	281 - 261 Bc	2nd June 261 Bc	"Antiochus The Saviour" Was A King Of The Hellenistic Seleucid Empire. He Succeeded His Father Seleucus 1 Nicator In 281 Bc And Reigned Until His Death On 02nd June 261 Bc. He Was The Last Known Ruler To Be Attributed The Ancient Mesopotamian Title King Of The Universe.

Kings of Ancient Greece

NAME:	D.O.B	REIGN	DIED	REASONS:
Lysimachus	360 Bce	306 - 281 Bce	281 Bce	He Was A Macedonian Officer And Diadochus (I.E "Successor" Of Alexander The Great, Who Became A Basileus ("King")In 306 Bc, Ruling Thrace, Asia Minor And Macedon.

REIGNING KINGS AND QUEENS IN THE BIBLE

Kings of Ancient Greece

NAME:	D.O.B	REIGN	DIED	REASONS:
Antiochus 1v Epiphanes	215/6 Bce	3 Sept 175 - Nov/Dec 164 Bce	164 Bce	He Was A Hellenistic King Of The Seleucid Empire From 175 Bc Until His Death In 164 Bc. He Was A Son Of King Antiochus 111 The Great. His Original Name Was Mithridates; He Assumed The Name Antiochus After He Ascended The Throne.

Other Reigning Kings and Princes

NAME:	D.O.B	REIGN	DIED	REASONS:
Herod Governor Of Galilee		Since 47 Bce		
Herod The King	73 Bce	37 - 04 Bce	04 Bce	He Reigned For 33 Years
Augustus Caesar	23rd Sept 63 Bce	16th Jan 27 Bce - 19th Aug 14 Ad	19th Aug 14 Ad	He Reigned For 40 Years And 7 Months
Tiberius Caesar Augustus	16th Nov 42 Bc	14 - 37 Ad	37 Ad	He Reigned For 53 Years
Jesus Christ	Betwee n 01 Bc/00bc & 00 Bc/00 Ad		30 Ad - 31 Ad	He Was Crucified.

A NOTE FROM THE AUTHOR

During Covid 19 lockdown, a few of my siblings, colleagues and I spent time studying the word of God. We began to study the word of God together on WhatsApp and then on Zoom.

My sister Christine was in Jamaica, my sister Avis in London and I in Grays, Essex. We first started to study the words of God and each chapter, line by line, and because we were in lockdown we had the time to get into the word of God each Monday to Friday evening for several hours.

After worshipping and praying together and asking the Holy Spirit to teach us His word, to give us knowledge, wisdom and understanding, God then opened up the scriptures to us and we were enjoying our study of the word of God so much that we were led into a deep knowledge of it. After a while, two of our church sisters in London then joined us when they could, and as time went by my niece and nephew in Birmingham then joined us too. Then we were also joined by another two of our church sisters in London. And so our little study group grew.

I discovered after a period of study and when listening back to our recorded lessons that I felt led to put our studies into writing. I then felt led to do the research and tie-up the word of God with world history. After doing the research I realised that many people do not understand much of the word of God and so I wanted as many as possible to be able to understand it like I now do.

I was brought up as a child in church - my parents were Christians and I got baptised in my late teens but was backslidden for a number of years. I came back to God after the death of my father in 1996. I attended many bible studies in church over the years but was not satisfied that I was always given the correct and full understanding of many of the scriptures. When we began to study during lockdown, I felt confident that I was being given the true meaning of many of God's words. I felt hunger and such a passion in my spirit to pass this knowledge on to as many people as seems possible.

I am now seventy two years old and would love these messages to go out to one and all. I feel that I have done what God wanted me to do and have now left it in the Hands of God. I hope you are blessed with further understanding of God's word from this book.

ELIZABETH BRUCE

Printed in Great Britain
by Amazon

53899249R00119